Coral Islanders

WORLDS
OF
MAN

Studies in
Cultural Ecology

EDITED BY
Walter Goldschmidt

University of California
Los Angeles

Coral Islanders

WILLIAM H. ALKIRE
UNIVERSITY OF VICTORIA, BRITISH COLUMBIA

AHM PUBLISHING CORPORATION
ARLINGTON HEIGHTS, ILLINOIS 60004

ISBN: 0-88295-618-3, cloth; ISBN: 0-88295-619-1, paper
Library of Congress Card Number: 77-90673

Printed in the United States of America
718

For Keiko

Foreword

Coral Islanders addresses the issue of cultural ecology from the perspective of environmental consistency. It recognizes that the tiny circlets dotting the South Pacific offer a special kind of environment and seeks to discover the social consequences of the conditions they impose.

The coral island is itself a fascinating phenomenon; an environment created by living organisms, a characteristic and lovely shape, white strands in a vast blue ocean—a proper backdrop for the romantic view that is the popular picture of the South Seas. The reality is far less idyllic. The soils are thin and poor in nutrition; fresh water is often scarce and may virtually disappear even when, in the words of the Ancient Mariner, water is everywhere. The low-lying lands are wracked by storms of great fury that destroy what man has wrought and often take much of the human population with them. It is a delicate environment that yields to human occupation only with the application of diligence and skill.

As matters turn out, coral islands by no means offer the uniform conditions that one is wont to ascribe to them. They vary in the degree to which they have adequate water and soil, in their vulnerability to storms and other environmental catastrophies, and these variations affect the character of the culture that is constructed upon them. But of all the factors that Alkire finds relevant, the most important for influencing human institutions is their relative degree of isolation. Some are set far from other inhabited land; some appear in clusters and still others are close to larger islands or land masses. That the degree of isolation should prove so important is not as surprising as may first appear. Human society is everywhere built upon collaborative effort, and the range of potential social interaction is affected by the size and variety of the population that is in a position to communicate with one another.

For this reason Alkire has classified the islands in terms of degree of isolation and examined aspects of their social organization in relation to this factor. He finds certain uniformities within each. In this way we not only know the degree of variation in island organization and social behavior, but come to appreciate the importance of the central factor of isolation. It is a factor long appreciated in the study of social behavior but, I believe, has not elsewhere been so carefully scrutinized.

In these atolls isolation takes on importance in relation to the natural hazards to which they are subject. Drought and storm influence both productivity and population. There is a cyclic pattern of population growth and decline, of economic well-being and economic hardship. The social institutions respond to these fluctuations, particularly those institutions related to population control, to the control of economic resources, and to the allocation of power and authority. The manner in which they cope with the demographic and economic consequences of hazard is directly related to the factor of isolation. For, those islands that are in interrelationship with others, particularly where there is internal diversity of ecological zones, have greater flexibility and hence greater continuity.

These matters are not merely of theoretical interest. Alkire points in his final chapter to the crucial importance of interisland communication and collaboration for the maintenance of a stable social and economic order under modern conditions.

Walter Goldschmidt

Preface

In writing this brief volume I have attempted not only to provide a comparative view of coral island societies from a slightly altered perspective, but also to produce a book that would be useful as a text supplement for students in an introductory anthropology course.

My own first-hand experience with coral island societies has been limited to those of the central and western Caroline Islands in Micronesia, specifically Lamotrek, Elato, Satawal, Woleai and Faraulep. Consequently I have relied on the published work of many other researchers in assembling data from other areas. I do not offer the result as a comprehensive study of Pacific coral island cultures. Such an objective would require many years of concentrated work. Rather, what has resulted is an analysis based on a representative sampling of coral island life and adaptive strategies. I am, of course, indebted to those scholars whose works are cited in the text and bibliography. I am hopeful that they will not be upset or outraged by any of my interpretations or possible misreadings of their data. Further I think it appropriate to apologize to those other scholars whose works I have failed to mention either because of the limitations of space or because in my research I have overlooked their contributions. The volume of literature on coral island societies has in the last few years experienced a minor information explosion and it is almost inevitable that some important studies have been missed in my review of the literature.

For those readers specifically interested in other comparative coral island studies I would certainly recommend the work of Leonard Mason (1968), Kenneth Knudson (1970) and the continuing series of volumes published by the Association for Social Anthropology in Oceania and the University Press of Hawaii. Much of the information on Woleai and Lamotrek demography that appears in this book was originally prepared for a paper delivered at a symposium on atoll populations at the East-West Center, Honolulu in December 1972 convened by Vern Carroll, then the editor of the above-named series.

I would like to thank Walter Goldschmidt, who originally suggested that I write this volume. I would also like to acknowledge gratefully the assistance I have received at various times from the following institutions: The National Institutes of Health, the National Science Foundation, and the Canada Council. These organizations financed my research, respectively, on Lamotrek, Woleai, and Faraulep. The University of Victoria provided a research grant that permitted preparation of many of the maps and charts contained herein. I thank Ms. Sharon Keen for the cartographic work.

William H. Alkire

Victoria, British Columbia
November 1977

Contents

Contents

INTRODUCTION

The characteristics of a coral island environment that are most often emphasized in descriptive accounts include limited land area, poor soils, low topography, few endemic species of flora or fauna, and great susceptibility to damage from storms or drought. Individually each of these features would tend to categorize this type of island as inhospitable to human settlements, while in combination they would seem to make permanent occupation all but impossible. One might be surprised then to discover that some coral islands support populations in excess of 1000 persons per square mile. Obviously, there must be some important counterbalancing environmental features present that permit this. Two such features are associated, in turn, with the geological structure of the islands and their tropical locale. First the majority of coral islands have a varied and rich marine resource inventory which follows from their extensive reef areas. Secondly, their poor soils notwithstanding, high yield horticulture is often possible because of the uniform tropical climate.

Perhaps the biggest mistake one could make when discussing coral islands would be to lapse into broad generalizations, for there are a large number of variables involved in this type of ecosystem. And this means there are a correspondingly large number of combinations and arrangements of these variables.

One must continually keep in mind that there is great variation among coral islands. Variation is a prime concern of this book, but so is generalization. Consequently the main focus throughout will be on those features of the traditional subsistence economies that reflect a successful adaptation to the realities of the environment.

In 1957 Ward Goodenough discussed the many advantages of examining problems of cultural evolution and cultural adaptation in an insular setting, a setting where variables and boundaries are more easily defined. In the twenty years that have followed numerous articles and monographs have appeared that have focused on these topics. Understandably most have dealt with the larger and more populous volcanic islands. Coral islands have been treated less satisfactorily, in part because they frequently have been relegated to a residual category in the cultural shadow of high island neighbors, from whom it was assumed they had inherited or adopted most of their cultural traits.

It is likely that the frequent failure to recognize distinctive patterns in coral island adaptations has resulted from not clearly defining the specifics of such ecosystems, from not identifying their systematic boundaries, and from assuming all were of one type. The variable of isolation is crucial in this context, and it is one that has often been underemphasized. In some cases, such as among the coral islands of Micronesia and Polynesia, a total ecosystem can be accurately defined as composed of a single raised coral island or atoll and its immediate surrounding sea, but in other cases the system can be adequately defined only if a multi-atoll configuration involving scores of islands and hundreds of square miles of reefs and lagoons is included. In the jargon of systems theory, the first case represents a relatively closed system while the second approximates a more open system. One could justifiably expect significant variation between the two systems, and it might be misleading or fruitless to search for complete uniformity. Consequently one assumption made in this book is that patterns of adaptation can be more easily defined and analyzed if particular societies are approached with such distinctions clearly in mind.

Chapter 1

CORAL ISLANDS

... everyone must be struck with astonishment, when he first beholds one of these vast rings of coral-rock, often many leagues in diameter, here and there surmounted by a lone verdant island with dazzling white shores, bathed on the outside by the foaming breakers of the ocean, and on the inside surrounding a calm expanse of water. . . .

Charles Darwin 1842

Coral reefs have been characterized as the oldest and most durable of the earth's ecosystems. Reefs containing true corals have been found that date back some 500 million years, and their complexity is reflected by the 80 different genera contained within their structure (Newell 1972).

Charles Darwin was the first naturalist to offer a comprehensive theory about the formation of coral islands and atolls. He was struck by the uniformity in structure of atolls, and by means of his *subsidence theory* he attempted to explain these similarities. On the whole his theory has withstood subsequent critical examinations with only minor modifications. Darwin hypothesized that most coral reefs began their growth on the offshore shelves of "ordinary islands," a term he used for volcanic islands, many of which were subsiding as a result of tectonic processes affecting the ocean floor (Figure 1a). The rate of subsidence was slow and the upward growth of coral, which has

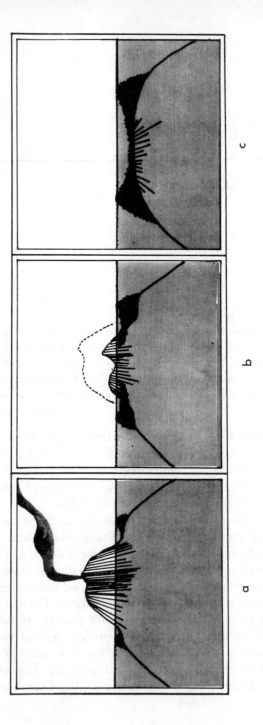

4

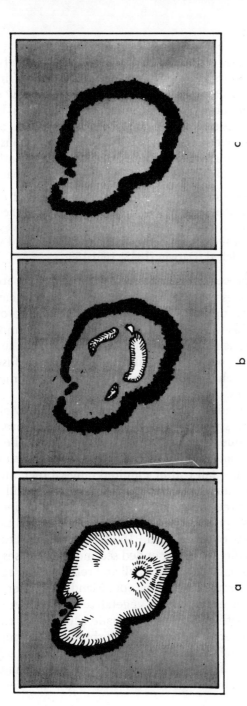

Figure 1 Darwin's Subsidence Theory: (a) coral reefs begin growth on the fringes of a subsiding volcanic island; (b) as the core island subsides the coral continues to grow and thus eventually reaches a stage where it forms a barrier reef encircling the remaining peaks of the core island; (c) an atoll reef remains after the volcanic core has disappeared below the surface.

since been variously estimated to proceed at a rate of between 5 and 14 millimeters per year, kept pace so that the fringing reefs eventually became barrier reefs, that is, reefs now some distance from the shore of the volcanic mass (Figure 1b). Eventually as the core island disappeared below the surface of the sea, the coral reef alone remained witness to the previous existence of the volcanic island (Figure 1c). His theory neatly accounted for many of the general similarities in atoll shape:

as atolls have been formed during the sinking of the land by the upward growth of the reefs which primarily fringed the shores of ordinary islands; so we might expect that these rings of coral . . . would still retain traces of the general form . . . of the islands round which they were first modelled (Darwin [1842] 1901:169).

The tectonic processes that resulted in subsidence apparently in certain instances reversed, so that sections of reef have in some places been uplifted or thrust above the surface of the ocean. In those cases where this has occurred, coral islands are now found rising as much as 200 or 300 feet above the surface of the surrounding ocean. These are the lone table-reef islands of the Pacific, which lack the lagoon and extended submerged reef areas of atolls.

The range of conditions under which the community of reef building organisms prosper has been defined more precisely since Darwin's time. It is a relatively narrow range. The temperature, clarity, and salinity of the water as well as sunlight penetration all must fall within a limited range if reef building is to occur. When subsidence is too rapid reef building will cease as the top of the reef descends below the maximum depth of adequate sunlight penetration, which under ideal conditions is estimated to be between 120 and 150 feet. A similar situation develops if turbidity from suspended sediments increases, perhaps the consequence of high rainfall and related rapid erosion carrying off mud from the volcanic core island. The latter could easily occur if, for example, the vegetative cover of an island were destroyed either through manmade activities or natural calamity; the consequent increase of turbidity in surrounding waters would cut off necessary sunlight, killing reefs or inhibiting their growth. Changes in water temperature, as can occur during localized alterations in currents, might also result in upwelling cold waters that could kill or inhibit reef growth. The tolerable range of temperature for coral growth is between 18° and 22° C. (64° to 72° F.). This fact not only .contributes to limiting the depth and distribution of live reefs but also limits the height of reef growth as it approaches the surface of the water, where temperature might rise above the tolerable limits. Thus it should be clear that the reef building system is, in itself, a relatively delicately balanced ecosystem.

The areas of the world where these necessary conditions are met and where they have for long periods of time been relatively constant are few, a point that Darwin made in his survey of 1842. Coral reefs and islands are found in the tropical areas of the Atlantic, Indian, and Pacific Oceans, but the reefs and islands of the Pacific are by far the most abundant.

Most of the coral islands, as contrasted to the more widely distributed reefs of the Pacific, are included in an arc extending east and southeast from the Caroline Islands of the Western Pacific through the Marshalls, Gilberts, Ellice, Phoenix, Tokelau, and Tuamotu archipelagoes (Map 1). Geological theories developed long after Darwin's time may eventually aid in explaining the distribution of atolls and raised coral islands. Plate tectonics and the processes of subduction and uplift may be one of the theories that will provide a model for understanding subsidence and uplift that have created at least some of the numerous atolls and table-reef islands of the Pacific.

If the variables thus far discussed—temperature and sunlight, sea water salinity and clarity, and subsidence—were constant and were the only ones influencing reef and atoll formation, one could expect the typical atoll to be composed primarily of live coral, circular in shape, lying a few feet below the surface of the sea. There would be very little likelihood that such a structure would have more than limited island-building properties. But salinity, clarity, subsidence, and temperature have all varied in the past, and, as outlined above, if these variations should cause reef building organisms to die, the reef invariably begins to break down under the forces of erosion. The resulting detritus provides the basic material necessary to form islets.

In the recent geological past the events of the Pleistocene are thought to have led to a period of extended atoll island building, not so much the result of lower water temperatures, since in

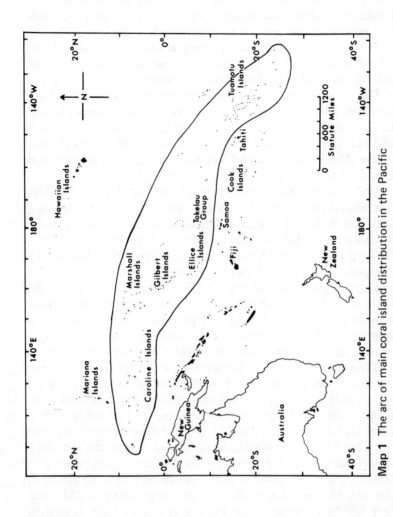

Map 1 The arc of main coral island distribution in the Pacific

many of the tropical areas of the Pacific temperatures of the sea water probably did not fall below a minimal 18° C., but rather because of the significant lowering of sea level during that era which exposed and killed large areas of reef. At the height of the Pleistocene it has been hypothesized that much of the earth's water was locked up in ice in the northern latitudes; so much water, in fact, that the general sea level of the Pacific was probably as much as 300 feet lower than at present. The reefs that consequently were exposed were subject to extended periods of wind and wave erosion, especially during tropical storms and typhoons. Much of the detritus resulting from this erosion accumulated along sheltered portions of the reef.

When sea levels once again began to rise at the end of the Pleistocene some of the detritus undoubtedly was washed away, either into the lagoon or into the open ocean; but other portions continued to accumulate on various parts of the reef. Herold Wiens (1962) found that points of curvature in the reef, for example, more often than not provided a degree of shelter from winds and currents so that detritus accumulated into the larger islets and islands. In post-Pleistocene times erosion of reefs continue but probably at a much reduced rate. Storm waves continue to break away small sections of living coral which subsequently are thrown up on the reef flat. Further, as the reef grows outward, the middle areas may, at low tides, be so protected that areas of stagnant sea water form where temperatures higher than that tolerated by live coral are common. As such areas die they too are increasingly subject to the forces of erosion. Certain biological processes may have similar effect. For example, the recently publicized attacks of crown-of-thorn starfish on tropical reefs in various parts of the Pacific, if repeated in history, may have led to reef death, erosion, and island building.

Some atoll islets never grow beyond a rudimentary accumulation of coral sand and cobbles. On the majority, however, if birds are present, if rainfall is adequate and if sea currents and winds are conducive, various types of vegetation soon take root. Such vegetation serves to anchor the islet and provides a stable environment that in turn increases the likelihood of continued growth in overall islet size. The first vegetation likely to take root under these marginal conditions are those hardy tropical varieties that are both salt and wind tolerant and that possess root structures capable of rapidly absorbing rainwater. Species of this type commonly found in the Pacific include such vines and shrubs as *Scaevola* and *Cassytha,* and strand tolerant bushes like *Pisonia, Pemphis, Messerschmidia,* and *Guettarda.* Pisonia is an ideal example in that it possesses attributes needed both for survival and for wide distribution. Its "sticky fruits are dispersed by birds (such as boobies) which often build their nests in Pisonias," and the plant is so tough that its "broken twigs may root if they fall in a suitable location" (Stone 1970: 273). Pandanus is probably one of the few trees with fruits useful as a food for man that is hardy enough to survive under similarly harsh conditions.

Coral island soils in the early phases of islet development are comparatively poor. They are made up of coral detritus and consequently are composed largely of calcium carbonate and magnesium carbonate. They form porous soils that are low in plant nutrients, especially iron. It is only after a layer of humus has accumulated, deposited by the early hardy varieties of vegetation, that a wider range of plants can survive. Since coralline soils, at least initially, are so poor, coral island vegetation is exceptionally dependent on water for sustenance.

The sole source of groundwater on an atoll islet is rain. The atoll island is distinguished by its flat topography, averaging little more than 6 or 8 feet above sea level. There are no springs or streams in this environment; and with no mountains to force convectional cooling of passing clouds, rainfall over the land averages no more than that falling on the surrounding ocean. In some areas this may, nevertheless, be high while in others it is quite low. In both cases that rain which does fall quickly percolates through the sand and cobbles and into the reef that lies below. The reef, although obviously porous, slows the dissipation of the fresh water into the surrounding sea and, because fresh water is less dense than salt water (a ratio of 40:41), a "lens" of fresh water (technically termed the *Ghyben-Hertzberg lens*) is formed, "floating" on the surface of the underlying seawater. This floating lens rises and falls with the tides. At the low points of an islet it may rise above the surface of the soil, while at other points of the islet it may be easily tapped through excavation of shallow wells. The purity of the water depends on the amount and frequency of rainfall and the size of the island, and, since the fresh water slowly dissipates into the surrounding sea, it must be continually replenished by frequent rain. The size of the lens and its longevity depends on the size of the islet —the larger the islet, the larger and slower the dissipation of its lens. An island less than 350 feet by 350 feet in area apparently is too small to develop a permanent Ghyben-Hertzberg lens.

With these points in mind, then, the range of vegetation one finds on an atoll islet is related to the amount and regularity of rainfall as well as islet size. Low or irregular rainfall introduces a drought factor, and islets subject to droughts can support only the hardiest, salt resistant strand species. Larger islets with heavy rainfall, evenly distributed throughout the year, may support three or four times as many species. By way of example, Canton Island in the Phoenix group lies in a low rainfall area of the Pacific, averaging only 19 inches of rain annually. The island supports a meagre total of fourteen species of flora. Arno atoll, in the Marshalls, on the other hand, averages some 160 inches of rain annually and supports some 125 species of vegetation (Wiens 1962: 364).

These same factors of rainfall and island size limit vegetation on raised coral islands as well, but, in addition, the elevation of this type of island may further restrict survival of vegetation. If such an island is uplifted more than a few feet above the ocean's surface, the possibility of tapping its freshwater lens becomes difficult for all vegetation except species with deep and penetrating root structures. Consequently even large raised coral islands often are covered only with limited strand vegetation, similar to that found on atoll islets too small to support permanent freshwater lenses. Furthermore, for the same basic reasons vegetation on raised coral islands is much more vulnerable to damage in times of drought. Sir Arthur Grimble, a long-time administrator in the Gilbert Islands, detailed a vivid picture of drought, its growth and self-perpetuating nature on Banaba, a raised coral island 300 miles west of the main chain of the Gilberts. He noted that fruit trees began to die after 6 months of drought, and after 12 months most of the coconut trees had also died, leaving the island naked to the sun "flinging back the savage heat in a white-hot column to heaven":

That soaring shaft of refraction stood like a pitiless sentinel on guard over the land. It was the barrier against which the rain clouds beat and were divided. When the westerly monsoon was due to begin, you could stand on the southwest point of the land and watch the black battalions riding up the sky towards you, trailing an unbroken curtain of rain across the sea's face below them. "At last!" you would say to yourself. "It's coming. It must be coming this time." And, as if to mock your hope, it would come so near you could hear the swish and whisper of it on the water. If you looked up then, you could see the cloud's edge sweep almost to the zenith. Almost, yet not near enough; in the last moment, you saw it waver, halt in the middle, torn apart there by the uprushing column of furnace-hot air. You watched its sundered halves pass by, spilling their torrents into the sea a few hundred yards from the coast on either hand, while, between them, under a sullen grey but rainless sky, the stricken land thirsted on (Grimble 1957: 34).

It is doubtful that a drought of similar length would be quite as disastrous on an atoll islet since some vegetation could survive by tapping the ground water lens, even though the lens would, through time, become more and more brackish. However, an atoll islet might suffer a similar decrease in rainfall if vegetation were removed or destroyed through some other agency, as might be the case in the event of a typhoon. The increased radiation heating of the atoll islet might then tend to decrease rainfall and inhibit post-typhoon recovery of vegetation on an atoll islet to the same extent as that described by Grimble on a raised coral island. There are, then, striking variations in vegetation between wet and dry coral islands, those subject to drought and those drought-free.

In general, rainfall is higher in the Western Pacific than in the Central or Eastern Pacific. The two belts of heaviest rainfall are located 5 to 10 degrees latitude on each side of the equator in the Western Pacific. Most of the coral islands of the Carolines lie in the northern belt of heavy precipitation where the average annual rainfall exceeds 120 inches. The Marshall Islands have similarly heavy precipitation except for those islands of the archipelago north of Wotje and Likiep—the average at Utirik, for example, is 70 inches annually and at Bikini, which lies 11° 30' North, it is less than 60 inches per year. Similarly, south of the equator one finds that in the northern Gilberts rainfall equals that of the Carolines. Butaritari receives between 120 and 140 inches annually. But as one moves farther south there is a continuous decrease, first to 61 inches on Tarawa and finally to some 30 or 40 inches per year at Tabituea. Banaba and Nauru, the two isolated raised coral islands west of the Gilberts, average approximately 80 inches precipitation per year, but, as the preceding passage from Grimble indicates, they also are subject to periodic and devastating droughts.

The rainfall averages for the Polynesian coral islands overall are lower than those of Micronesia, lying as they do in the generally less wet Eastern Pacific. The Tokelau and Northern Cook islands receive between 100 and 115 inches per year, but seasonally distributed so that the dry season, between May and September, results in a short annual drought. The Phoenix and southern Line Islands have one of the lowest averages of the insular Pacific, less than 30 inches. The Tuamotu archipelago overall averages range from 45 to 60 inches per year.

Tropical storms with their accompanying high winds are a second source of environmental stress for vegetation on coral islands. The prevailing winds throughout most of the tropical Pacific are the tradewinds—northeast trades in the northern hemisphere and southeast trades in the southern hemisphere. The reliability of these winds in the equatorial regions varies, however, as the intertropical convergence zone seasonally moves from northern to southern hemispheres. Consequently, these regions seasonally experience more frequent calms and variable winds than other areas of higher latitudes. In the Western Pacific tropical storms are most frequently generated in the vicinity of the convergence zone at the time of the year when it is firmly established either north or south of the equator. In the northern hemisphere this occurs in the period between July and October and in the southern hemisphere, December through March. Wiens has commented on this phenomenon as follows:

The marked concentration of intense typhoon developments during the late summer and fall may be related to the maximum accumulation of heat at the latter part of the summer half-year in each hemisphere. This should lead to a higher rate of evaporation and higher moisture content in the atmosphere. A greater amount of moisture is then available for condensation in the convectional currents in the equatorial trough. Hence, there should be greater energy releases with convectional movements, leading to the increased turbulence that develops into cyclones (Wiens 1962: 174).

This seasonal distribution of typhoons or hurricanes is not unfailing however, and such storms can occur in either hemisphere in nearly any month of the year. The coral islands that are most seriously and frequently affected by these storms are those of Micronesia, especially those of the central and western Carolines. The so-called breeding ground for north Pacific typhoons is in the vicinity of the Truk Islands, although tropical storms may originate in the same latitudes as far east as the Marshall or Gilbert archipelagoes. These storms generally follow a track that carries them west and northwest toward the Philippines, Japan, and the Asian mainland. Consequently, those coral islands that lie between Truk and Yap are the ones most frequently damaged by the accompanying high winds.

The hurricanes that originate south of the equator generally have their genesis in the oceanic areas between Samoa and the New Hebrides. These storms tend to move south and southeast thus missing most areas of coral island concentration, although they frequently wreak havoc on the volcanic islands of the region. As was the case in the north, storms can and do develop outside this area and these occasionally do affect some of the coral islands of the south Pacific, for example, the Ellice or Tuamotus.

A typhoon, the winds of which by definition are in excess of 75 miles per hour, obviously can devastate a coral island. In fact any tropical storm with winds of 45 miles per hour will cause some damage to the unprotected vegetation of the low flat atoll islet. The 100 mile per hour winds and storm waves of a typical typhoon destroy vegetation, may raise sea level 15 to 20 feet above normal and thus displace the fresh water lens, and seriously erode atoll islets. Even in those areas of high rainfall it may take the vegetation of a coral island six to ten years to recover completely from the damage of a severe tropical storm.

Figure 2 attempts, albeit in a highly simplified manner, to arrange systematically the major variables thus far mentioned: island area, elevation, rainfall and the two most important sources of environmental stress, droughts and typhoons. Soils have been omitted from consideration at this point since on most coral islands they vary mainly in texture—those that are coarser having generally been less exposed to the forces of erosion—rather than in content. The organic and mineral con-

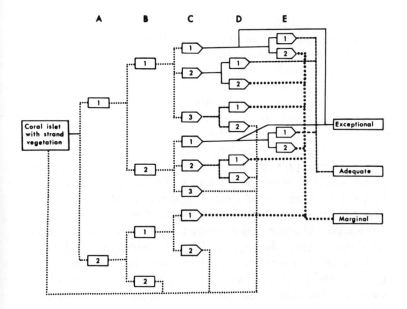

Column A = Island size
1. Island more than 350' X 350'.
2. Island less than 350' X 350'.
Column B = Island elevation
1. Average elevation less than 20' above sea level.
2. Average elevation more than 20' above sea level.
Column C = Rainfall
1. Average annual rainfall more than 80".
2. Average annual rainfall between 35" and 80".
3. Average annual rainfall less than 35".
Column D = Droughts
1. Frequency no more than 1 every 5 to 10 years.
2. Frequency 1 or more every 4 to 5 years.

Column E = Typhoons
1. Average frequency less than 1 every 5 to 10 years.
2. Average frequency more than 1 every 4 to 5 years.
Lines to cells indicating potential support/survival of human communities:
  Solid line—combination of variables suggests exceptional support.
  Dashed line—combination of variables suggests adequate support.
  Heavy dotted line—combination of variables suggests marginal support.
  Light dotted line—combination of variables suggests inadequate or no support.

Figure 2 Factors influencing coral island vegetative growth and potential support of human occupation.

tent is a consequence of the presence or absence of vegetation, which is, of course, related to the interaction of these other variables on a particular island.

Beginning with the single compartment at the left of the diagram, which represents a coral island or islet with a minimum of strand vegetation (say, ten or fewer species of hardy vines, shrubs, and bushes), one proceeds to the right along the paths of the diagram leading to cells in the next two columns, representing specific varieties of such islands. The next three columns contain decision function cells representing the major variables external to the islet itself that fundamentally influence vegetation life and growth. Finally, the terminal compartments are labeled, following the accumulated characteristics of the paths leading to them, according to the potential such islets possess to support human habitation.

COLUMN A: AREA. Island size is crucial in the formation of a permanent ground water lens and this is a necessary prerequisite for the support of a wide range of vegetation. The smallest islet capable of developing a lens will be no less than 350 feet by 350 feet (Tracey *et al* 1961: 35); an islet about 3 acres in size. The two compartments in this column therefore represent islets above and below this dividing line, but it should be emphasized that in this column, as well as all others, it would be more meaningful to conceive of a continuum rather than isolated types if one is to represent accurately the full range of islet variation. The compartments here represent points on that continuum.

COLUMN B: ELEVATION. Most vegetation will only have access to ground water if such water does not lie too far below the surface. The small cell 2 (hereafter represented $\boxed{2}$, keyed to Figure 2), raised coral islands with an average elevation greater than 20 feet above sea level will probably not support more than a basic inventory of strand vegetation. An atoll islet of similar size, however, even if it does not possess a fully developed Ghyben-Hertzberg lens, might sustain a wider range of species if located in a high rainfall area. The low elevation of this island type would permit the root systems of most plants easier access to any ground water that even temporarily was present. Thus an island of type $\boxed{2.2}$ is more limited in potential than one of type $\boxed{2.1}$. Using this notational convention, then, an island with a "cell" designation made up of a series of low numbers has greater potential productivity than one including one or more high numerals.

COLUMN C: RAINFALL. Since seasonal distribution of rain is nearly as important as annual totals one must be cautious when proposing threshholds for vegetation survival based on annual figures. Nevertheless, at the lower end of the scale, any coral island that receives less than 30 inches per year, no matter how evenly distributed such rainfall is throughout the year, probably will not retain enough moisture to support more than 15 or 20 plant species. Wake atoll, for example, supported between 16 and 20 species on 30 to 40 inches annual precipitation. Bikini, with a moderate rainfall between 60 and 70 inches annually, possessed 58 species; while Arno, an atoll in the same chain had an inventory of 100 to 125 plant species and high rainfall, averaging more than 100 inches per year. Three cells are provided in the diagram representing high, medium, and low rainfall at the approximate levels of more than 80 inches, 35 to 80 inches, and less than 35 inches, respectively.

COLUMN D: DROUGHT. Grimble (1957:34) estimated that droughts on Banaba occurred once every seven or eight years. While rainfall in non-drought years on this island probably averages in the vicinity of 80 inches per year, the frequency of droughts means that only a limited number of plant species are able to survive these times of stress. Consequently, when the island was inhabited many plant species had to be reintroduced from neighboring areas after severe droughts. It seems reasonable to assume then, with Banaba as a baseline, that under conditions where droughts were more frequent than once every five years only the hardiest of strand species would survive. The two cells of the column therefore represent contrasting drought conditions: (1) droughts of no greater frequency than one every five to ten years; and (2) serious drought conditions, with a frequency of one every four to five years.

COLUMN E: TYPHOONS. Vegetation destroyed by a severe typhoon may also require five to seven years for recovery. Any single coral island subjected to severe storms more frequently than this could support to maturity only hardy wind and salt tolerant species. Two cells are similarly provided in the diagram representing these contrasting conditions.

From the perspective of vegetation growth and survival potential, then, the ideal coral island is classified as $\boxed{1.1.1}$ on this diagram if factors of environmental stress are absent or $\boxed{1.1.1.1}$ if a limited number of tropical storms occur. At the other extreme are the proverbial "desert islands," $\boxed{2.2.3}$ or $\boxed{2.2.3.2}$, both of which have been omitted from the diagram in the interests of schematic clarity and economy.

Growth potential, however, is not tied in any direct way to

the actual introduction of plant species. Variables external to the diagrammed system play crucial roles here. Relative isolation, prevailing winds, ocean currents, flight patterns and habits of birds and, perhaps the most important, the presence of human communities and contact must be examined in order to understand the introduction and distribution of floral types in the insular Pacific.

The faunal resources of coral islands and atolls are a study in contrasts—a meagre terrestrial inventory and a rich marine assemblage. The relative isolation brought about by the wide expanses of water between many of the island chains of Polynesia and Micronesia apparently severely restricted the dispersal of land fauna into these two regions just as these same factors limited the spread of flora. The terrestrial fauna inventory, in fact, is almost non-existent when compared with neighboring Melanesia. In both Micronesia and Polynesia the bat was the only land mammal that predated man's arrival and even it was not present on all coral islands. A variety of oceanic bird species was present, but in most cases it included only 15 or 20 species. Terrestrial crabs and a variety of lizards were the only other common species. Before man's arrival there were no pigs, dogs, chickens, or rats; and in some cases, at least, no mosquitoes or flies.

The reefs and surrounding waters of coral islands, on the other hand, provided shelter and ample food for a profusion of marine species. By way of example, in both the Gilberts and Tuamotus some 400 different species of reef and pelagic fishes have been identified. Shellfish and turtles were also present and often numerous in this undisturbed setting.

These are the variables and ranges of conditions that confronted the first human colonists arriving on a Pacific coral island. The combination of variables in any particular case and the process of cultural adaptation usually determined whether such colonists gained a foothold and prospered or whether the community was destined for extinction or forced abandonment of the island.

Chapter 2

SETTLEMENT, SURVIVAL, AND GROWTH

Man as a component in the wider ecosystem of coral reef life is decidedly a newcomer, probably entering the picture no more than 3 or 4 thousand years ago. Very little archaeological work has been done on coral islands; consequently, the dates of original settlement for particular islands and archipelagoes that have been proposed are approximations usually based on archaeological evidence from neighboring volcanic islands. In some cases even this kind of evidence is lacking, and, thus, settlement dates and migration routes have been proposed using linguistic similarities and dialect chains as evidence.

The first movements into the Pacific involved a slow infiltration of bands of nomadic hunters and gatherers from the Asian and Southeast Asian mainland into Indonesia, New Guinea, and possibly Australia (Shutler and Shutler 1975). This transpired over a long span of time beginning some 40,000 years ago, at which time large parts of Indonesia were connected to the mainland by land bridges that emerged during the lower sea levels of the Pleistocene. Even so, the smaller and more distant islands and certainly the coral islands were not settled until a much later date. In fact many of the latter were probably still in early stages of formation, possessing little vegetation and even less fauna, and thus were unsuitable for a people following a hunting and gathering mode of subsistence. The successful colonization of coral islands required human communities with a developed technology of horticulture, marine exploitation, and seafaring.

The archaeological work of Alexander Spoehr (1957) and Douglas Osborne (1966) suggests that both Yap and Palau in western Micronesia were settled by 1500 B.C., probably by immigrants from the Philippines and Indonesia. There is no evidence, however, that the coral islands of Micronesia were inhabited by a similarly early date. The small amount of archaeology that has been done in central and eastern Micronesia, where most of the coral islands are found, has not been directed towards answering questions about original settlement. Consequently hypotheses on this topic have relied heavily on linguistics for supporting evidence. These studies have shown that the languages of central and eastern Micronesia have their closest correlates in the Fiji–New Hebrides region of Melanesia (Grace 1961; Dyen 1965). The radiocarbon dates obtained from this area of eastern Melanesia indicate that these islands were occupied sometime before 800 B.C. These pieces of linguistic and archaeological information imply a population movement into eastern and central Micronesia from eastern Melanesia, the latter area also being the general region from which other migrants set out for Polynesia. Much more extensive archaeological data are available from Polynesia, but even this relates primarily to volcanic rather than coral islands. It is now well established that the high islands of Polynesia were colonized over a longer period of time, stretching from approximately 1000 B.C. in the west to 1200 A.D. in some areas of the east (Bellwood 1975).

Some authors have suggested that most of the coral islands of the Pacific were only inhabited after all the nearby volcanic islands had been settled (Howells 1973). The rationale for this theory is that, given a choice, no community would voluntarily choose the poorer environmental setting of a low island over the richer potential of a high island. This may be a reasonable assumption in those areas of the Pacific where volcanic and coral islands are in close association, such as the Society Islands and the Tuamotus. There are a number of coral islands and coral island chains, however, quite isolated from any volcanic neighbors—the Marshalls, Gilberts, and Ellice Islands for example—and, consequently, there was no real choice between high and low island. Furthermore it is conceivable that settlers whose origins lay in Melanesia might prefer what they would assume to be the generally healthier coral islands to presumed malarial high islands when moving into the unknown areas of both Micronesia and Polynesia. Once a population has adapted to coral island life, in some instances the attractions of their richer marine resources might outweigh the greater horticultural possibilities of volcanic islands, especially if such horticultural possibilities could only be realized after several years of backbreaking work. Without concrete archaeological evidence discussions of chronological order of settlement are obviously speculative, but it seems likely that the coral islands were occupied at essentially the same time as their volcanic counterparts. For the coral islands of eastern Polynesia this means a time period ranging from 500 A.D. to 1500 A.D.

The linguistic diversity of Micronesia and the period of time it would take to produce such diversity among fundamentally related languages suggest that most of the coral islands were occupied or known and exploited by the sixteenth century when the first Europeans arrived in the area. The atolls of the Gilberts, Marshalls, and eastern Carolines were probably settled between 100 A.D. and 1000 A.D. Those of the central Carolines may have been colonized somewhat later, but undoubtedly most by 1300 A.D., since there is historic evidence that all of the islands of the central Carolines presently inhabited were also settled at the latest by 1664 (Krämer 1917: 4).

Throughout the Pacific, then, man has been influenced by and has been altering the coral atolls and islands for at least the past 700 to 800 years. Although there are significant environmental differences among many of these islands and atolls, many of the basic problems of initial adaptation and survival are similar enough to justify some generalizations about the likely processes initial settlers followed.

The early colonists of the Western Pacific were usually made up of small groups of voyagers, perhaps no more than one or two canoes full of individuals, who happened upon a previously unoccupied island. The folklore and history of Oceania are replete with stories of such canoes drifting ashore on both inhabited and uninhabited islands (Golson 1962; Riesenberg 1965). In the western Carolines, for example, the present day inhabitants of Sonsoral, a raised coral island south of Palau, trace their origins to a group of ancestral survivors of one or more canoes that had drifted to the island from Ulithi. Merir, Pulo Ana, and Tobi were later discovered and settled from Sonsoral in the course of short voyages from that island.

Some voyagers may have specifically set sail in search of new lands. Since the early colonists were entering Micronesia and Polynesia from the land-dotted regions of Melanesia, it is quite likely that their "world view" of the Pacific was one of a land-filled sea (Levison, Ward, and Webb 1973). Other voyagers undoubtedly made their discoveries when unexpectedly blown off course during storms while travelling between known points. In either case the coral islands thus discovered were as described in the previous chapter, initially land and vegetation poor, but often rich in marine resources. If there was little hope or desire on the part of such travellers to return to their island of origin, an attempt would probably be made to settle permanently the newly discovered island. Survival depended not only on the particular combination of environmental variables present, but also on how successfully the colonists exploited this potential. One advantage Pacific voyagers possessed was a technological inventory (or knowledge of such) adapted to the realities of insular living. As one example of this fact, archaeological evidence from the volcanic New Hebrides demonstrates that its residents were utilizing shell adzes and axes nearly identical to those found on the coral islands of Micronesia (Shutler and Shutler 1975). If such New Hebridean tool types predate those of Micronesia (no dates are yet available) it could indicate a simple and direct transfer of at least one basic tool type from a high island environment to that of coral islands where no other alternative was possible, since volcanic stone was absent.

Shells for adzes, axes, and scrapers were abundant on coral islands. Various fibers and vines were also readily available for manufacture of twines, ropes, and clothing, as well as adequate small timber for other tools, canoes, and housing needs. Houses, for example, were generally simple structures that could easily be built with available materials which might be limited on the smaller islands. In the coral islands of the central and western Carolines, for example, houses were built directly on the ground or on low coral stone platforms. These are described in greater detail in the next chapter.

The basic construction materials and techniques were similar throughout the coral islands of Micronesia and Polynesia, although specific shapes, floor plans, and decoration varied from one island group to another. In the past many of the larger structures utilized stone houseposts made from slabs of beach rock, a form of consolidated coral sand, gravel, and cobbles commonly found along the shoreline of the ocean side of a atoll islet. Some of these houseposts can still be seen standing on the islands of the central Carolines. A few writers have viewed these remains as evidence of influences from an ancient "megalithic" complex of Asian mainland origin. These artifacts can be accounted for somewhat less colorfully by considering the resources available on coral islands during the period of initial occupation and subsequently at times of maximum population. In both cases trees large enough to furnish houseposts for such structures were undoubtedly either too rare or too valuable for other purposes—for example as fruit-bearing trees or as potential timber for canoe construction—to sacrifice to house construction when an abundant alternative such as beach rock was readily available.

In addition to housing, the apparatus of marine exploitation and gardening and the inventory of other tools directly related to food production were of great importance to pioneering coral island residents. In most cases the canoes, hooks, lines, traps, weirs, and nets of the coral island cultures of Polynesia and Micronesia had their antecedents in Melanesian and Indonesian forms. Differentiation began from the time of first separation, however, as the various colonists adapted to the realities of each particular island and the most efficient system of marine exploitation. Canoe types provide an interesting example of this process of divergence.

Oceanian canoes are constructed with four basic parts: keel section, strakes, end pieces, and outrigger. A. C. Haddon and John Hornell (1936) have recorded the variation in design of each of these parts and the assembled whole throughout Oceania. Items of material culture, just as languages, begin to diverge in form and function as their carriers disperse and become isolated. In the case of Oceanian canoes, there is wide variation from area to area related both to availability of materials for construction and intended primary function of the craft. For example, one notes the development of double outriggers in Indonesia, large paddling canoes in Melanesia, double canoes in Polynesia, and asymmetrical sailing canoes in Micronesia. In many ways the large paddling and double canoes of Polynesia seem closer in form and function to their probable Melanesian prototypes than either is to the technically specialized sailing canoes of Micronesia.

Some of the variation within these major types of craft is probably related to differing sea and island conditions. For example, low island canoes, when compared with canoes from neighboring volcanic islands, often display a significant difference in the quality and specific characteristics of construction materials. Whereas there is usually adequate or even an abundance of timber on the larger Polynesian and Micronesian high islands, timber is in constant short supply on nearly every coral island. Consequently on many of the high islands large canoes may be hewn from a single log, with only narrow wash strakes and decorative end pieces added to the single piece hull. A canoe of this design basically is a long, shallow draft paddling canoe. When two such hulls are joined together in a double canoe, as was commonly done on Hawaii, Tonga, Samoa, and Tahiti, a craft with ocean-going and sailing capabilities results. In contrast the canoes of coral islands are generally smaller and of these only the smallest paddling canoes have hulls constructed of a single piece. Since on most canoes it is desirable to have a single piece keel for strength, coral island canoes are limited in overall length by the available timber. Few are more than 40 or 45 feet long and all but the smallest have a number of strakes sewn with sennit twine to the keel section and to each other up to gunwale height. Their design is one of a shorter, deeper keeled craft, as illustrated in Figure 3.

Variations from the basic design are related to specific uses. For example on Woleai there are twelve different kinds of canoes. Five are varieties of paddling canoes, designed to carry from one to five or more paddlers. The three smallest are meant for use within the lagoon and along the shore; the two larger are designed for use outside the lagoon, along the reef. There are six varieties of sailing canoes, two designated for travel and

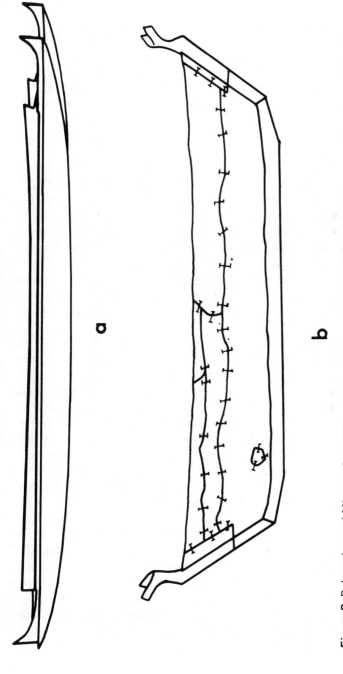

a

b

Figure 3 Polynesian and Micronesian sailing canoe profiles. (a) Typical profile of a Polynesian (Hawaiian) double canoe. Note the shallow draft design. (b) Typical profile of a Micronesian (Carolinian) sailing canoe. Note deep draft design and strake construction.

25

fishing inside the lagoon, two for trolling outside the lagoon, and two designed for open ocean inter-island travel. And finally there is one craft that is exclusively used on ceremonial occasions. All of these have the same basic design, but each incorporates a number of refinements suited to its intended use.

The horticultural tool inventory of early settlers on coral islands was undoubtedly simpler than the tool inventory of marine exploitation. It can be itemized as follows: knives and axes for clearing land, digging sticks and hoes for planting and cultivation, harvesting poles (for breadfruit and pandanus), a variety of baskets for transport or storage, and coconut-husking sticks and scrapers for food preparation. All of these implements had antecedent forms in other areas of Oceania, but were manufactured with materials locally available. As indicated in the previous chapter, there were few endemic coral island plants suitable for cultivation when colonists first arrived on any particular coral island. Pandanus and coconuts in some instances may have been present before humans, but more commonly most of the food plants were introduced by the colonists themselves.

At the time of European discovery the coral islanders of Micronesia and Polynesia depended on one or more of such cultivars as coconuts, pandanus, Cyrtosperma, Colocasia, Alocasia, and breadfruit. Crops of minor importance included sugar cane, arrowroot, Crataeva, and bananas. A number of these were introduced by the first migrants, while the others arrived as a result of post-settlement travel and commerce. Of course a number of cultivated plants currently important were introduced directly and indirectly in post-European contact times: sweet potatoes (in most cases), papayas, lemons, limes, peppers, squash, and tobacco are the most widely distributed and important of this class.

The earliest crops that were introduced on a newly discovered island were naturally those most frequently carried as stores aboard travelling canoes, and, this being the case, they would not have had to be specially stocked with the intention of undertaking a voyage of discovery. The problems of propagation after arrival at a previously uninhabited island varied, a fact made clear in chapter 1. Pandanus and coconuts could be planted and grown under all but the most extreme conditions.

Both are salt-tolerant species, but, even so, after planting it is unlikely that either would bear fruit before five to seven years had passed. Cyrtosperma and Colocasia are both root crops, collectively termed aroids, that could be harvested after eight or twelve months of growth, but both would have required intensive care if they were to survive in the initially poor soils of coral islands. They grow best in wet and swampy settings where humus content is high. Although some atoll islets, especially those located at bends of the reef, possess natural swamps, many others do not. In these latter instances before Colocasia or Cyrtosperma could be grown, swampy areas had to be excavated to a level where the water lens could easily be tapped by the plants. In either case mulching would have been required to increase the humus content of the coral-line soils.

A canoe load of colonists, then, would have been dependent on the indigenous resources of an island until such time as those plants they themselves introduced began to bear fruit. Unquestionably marine products played an even more important part in survival during those early years of settlement than in later years. There are a number of atolls today, poor in land resources, that have exploitation patterns and emphases which probably closely parallel these early patterns of subsistence. Michael Levin's recent work on Eauripik, an atoll of the western Carolines with a total land area of 0.09 square miles and a population of about 146, for example, found that marine resources were the critical staple on this small atoll. Ward Goodenough noted a similar dependence in the southern Gilbert Islands, where pandanus and coconuts are the only crops able to survive the low rainfall and periodic droughts. In both of these cases fish were the dietary staple and copra or pandanus the supplementary "side-dish."

There are, however, a number of other coral islands, especially raised coral islands, in both Micronesia and Polynesia with poor fisheries. The populations of these islands by necessity were and are almost totally dependent on gardening for sustenance. Fais is one such example. This raised coral island has only a limited reef area contiguous to the island, which itself is 1.10 square miles in area. The 1973 population was 213 individuals who were primarily dependent on sweet potato gardening for food. Fais has so few marine resources that the population hunts and consumes sharks, a fact that makes the island the butt of many jokes by the residents of neighboring atolls where the idea of eating a shark is near anathema. Survival on an island of this type during the early years of settlement was probably precarious and population growth more limited than on many smaller but resource-richer atolls.

Most coral islands of the Pacific, of course, fall somewhere between the two extremes of near total dependence on marine resources, on the one hand, and near total reliance on land production, on the other. Since the available land for gardening is not as severely limited nor the populations as dense as in the case of Eauripik, the majority of coral islanders derived a higher percentage of their food from gardening activities than from marine exploitation.

McArthur, Saunders, and Tweedie (1976) have demonstrated with computer simulations that even in colonization situations involving as few as six individuals, three males and three females, there is a fifty-fifty probability that the community could successfully establish itself and survive for at least 500 years and probably indefinitely into the future. Theoretically, given a population with normal sex and age distributions, an island probably would have to be able to support a minimal population of 30 to 50 individuals in order to reproduce itself over an indefinite period of time. If this population were distributed in a somewhat idealized manner one could assume it contained 50 percent males and 50 percent females. Forty-five percent of the population would be below 15 years of age, 42 percent between 16 and 44 years of age (the prime reproductive and physically active years), and 13 percent 45 years of age and over. Converted to actual numbers in a community of 30 to 50 individuals, this would result in 13 to 22 children 15 years of age and younger, 12 to 22 potentially active adults and 4 to 7 old people.

The survival of the community would depend primarily on the labor of 6 to 10 adult males and an equal number of females ranging in age from 16 to 44. A community with fewer adults could easily be faced with ultimate extinction if tragedy and natural disaster struck. The loss of a canoe load of fishermen, a number of deaths during an epidemic or warfare, in combination with drought or typhoon damage, might endanger the survival of the whole community by removing essential elements of the labor force and the core of the reproductive members.

How large would a coral island have to be to support our presumed minimal viable community of 30 to 50 individuals? Eauripik is probably near this minimum size. Olimarao, another atoll also in the Carolines, is slightly smaller, with a land area of 0.08 square miles. It once was inhabited but was abandoned in the 1800s following a devastating typhoon.

Given these realities of Eauripik and Olimarao, the assumptions just stated, and the variables discussed in chapter 1, it seems reasonable to assume that even under ideal circumstances an islet no smaller than 0.05 square miles in total area with an exploitable area of 15 to 20 acres and a lagoon or reef area equivalent to 1 square mile in area would be necessary to support a community of 50. And if the island in question were subject to any of the environmental stresses discussed in the previous chapter, the community might have to be considerably larger to guarantee survival. There is evidence, for example, that Malden and Fanning atolls in the Line Islands were once inhabited. Malden has an area of some 15 square miles and an enclosed shallow lagoon, while Fanning Island is approximately 13 square miles in area with 43 square miles of lagoon. Annual precipitation on Fanning has totaled as high as 100 inches, but on Malden it is generally less than 30 inches. Both islands are subject to droughts. In the course of an archaeological survey Kenneth Emory (1934) counted 37 house sites and several large kitchen middens on Malden. Both islands however had been abandoned before the time of European discovery. Emory estimated that Malden had supported a community of between 100 and 200 individuals. Seven ancient shallow wells were discovered but none contained water. This scarcity of water, resulting from both low rainfall and frequent droughts, probably led to the abandonment of the island.

The carrying capacity of an atoll islet that receives adequate rainfall can be surprisingly high (see Bayliss-Smith, 1974, for a comprehensive discussion of carrying capacity on coral atolls). Very dense populations could be supported by horticulture alone. For example, the relatively small atoll of Lamotrek, with a total land area of 0.24 square miles currently sustains a population of 233 individuals. The atoll receives between 100 and 130 inches of rain per year, which means there is a well developed fresh water lens. In the center of the main island of the atoll there is an extensive low lying swampy area covering 58 acres which is devoted to Cyrtosperma and Colocasia cultivation. The estimated annual yield of these aroids in the intensively culti- vated portions of the swamp is 15,000 pounds per acre, which is equal to yields of these same crops on some of the volcanic islands of Melanesia (Barrau 1958: 42). This figure is not unique among atolls, either, as Tim Bayliss-Smith estimated a similar yield per acre on Ontong-Java. In the case of Lamotrek it is estimated that this level of productivity could support as many as 25 to 27 persons per acre. Degener (1930: 81) estimated that Colocasia cultivation in aboriginal Hawaii supported 24 persons per acre. Under ideal conditions, then, aroid cultivation on atolls will produce yields as high, and support populations as dense, as commonly found under aboriginal conditions on the volcanic islands of Melanesia and Polynesia. In fact the level of productivity ranks high on any world scale of non-mechanized agriculture (for example, Lawton 1973).

If subsistence depends primarily on coconuts, a much less dense population can be maintained. A mature coconut tree bears between 100 and 300 nuts per year. An atoll islet with rainfall of 100 or more inches per year could support an average of 70 to 80 bearing trees per acre. Ernest Beaglehole estimated that an average individual subsisting on coconuts consumes be- tween seven and ten nuts per day. An acre of land planted in coconuts thus would support eight to ten people. Our hypothet- ical minimal community of 50 would thus require 2 to 5 acres of intensively cultivated Cyrtosperma or 5 to 10 acres of coco- nut trees in order to survive with a modest surplus for emergen- cies.

These two classes of food crops—aroids and coconuts—pos- sess some similar advantages as staples for island populations. They are both perennial and, upon maturity, continue to yield fruit all year. The aroids can be left in the ground until needed, and when they are harvested the top of the corm is neatly trimmed and replanted where it will again begin to grow. Coco- nut palms are hardy trees that yield fruits for 20 or more years. With these non-seasonal characteristics, there is little need for storage facilities or preservation techniques. In a sense the taro field and coconut grove are gardens and storehouses at one and the same time. Pandanus and breadfruit lack this advantage as subsistence crops. Both are seasonal and although neither requires greater care in cultivation than the coconut palm, some system of food preservation and storage is required if a population is to subsist all year on either. Preservation techniques were developed in many cases. Breadfruit is commonly fermented and stored in leaf- and mat-lined earthen pits. Pandanus is often stored as dried flour or is occasionally smoked.

Very few coral island communities, if they have a choice, depend on a single subsistence crop. Their horiculture is diversified just as their marine exploitation techniques are diversified, so that all contingencies can be met and successfully overcome. On most islands where conditions permit even if nuts or aroids are the staple, one also finds pandanus, breadfruit, sweet potatoes, arrowroot, and bananas grown. During times of drought, or following a typhoon, one of these secondary crops can rapidly become a staple. Population growth and densities ultimately are tied to the carrying capacity of specific coral islands. As Table 1 shows, population density figures vary widely among the coral islands of Micronesia and Polynesia, and much of this variability is related to the individual characteristics and carrying capacity of specific islands. This will be discussed in more detail in chapter 4.

The 1974 census of the Trust Territory of the Pacific Islands, which includes most of the islands of Micronesia, indicates that the population of these islands is growing at an annual rate of 3.5 percent. Although this reflects a birth rate probably somewhat higher than that experienced in traditional times, there is evidence that in pre-contact times densities were also high, and many coral island societies actively had to face and deal with problems of overpopulation. One of the earliest recorded statements about the central Caroline coral islands, for example, dates from 1664. In that year some 30 Carolinian canoes drifted to the Philippines. The Jesuit missionaries in the Philippines were told by the voyagers of some 50 islands from whence they came that were "as populated as an anthill" (Krämer 1917: 4). An interesting aspect of coral island populations, however, given the small land areas and small total population numbers

Table 1 Population densities for selected Coral Islands of Micronesia and Polynesia

Island	Area (sq. mi.)	Present Approx. Population	Density (Persons/ sq. mi.)
Nauru	7.70	4000	520
Kapingamarangi	0.52	500	1200
Niue	100.00	5000	50
Tongareva	6.00	610	100
Pukapuka	2.00	760	380
Rakahanga	1.50	329	220
Manihiki	2.00	556	278
Raroia	8.00	175	22
Nukunonu	2.00	553	275
Fakaofo	1.00	733	366
Eauripik	0.09	146	1411
Lamotrek	0.38	233	613
Elato	0.20	48	160
Fais	1.10	213	194
Satawal	0.50	354	708
Woleai	1.75	644	347
Faraulep	0.16	149	762

involved, is that on some islands, at least, a problem of over-population can easily and rapidly be replaced by a problem of underpopulation. Data from Woleai and Lamotrek atolls serve to illustrate some of the many factors that can influence population growth and decline on small islands.

Freycinet in the early 1800s estimated the population of Lamotrek atoll to be 2000 (Table 2). If this estimate were any-where near accurate (which admittedly is doubtful) it meant a density of 5277 persons per square mile. Shortly before this time Wilson estimated the population of Woleai from a ship-board observation in the following way:

About sixty canoes came off at first, and afterwards some of our people counted one hundred fifty in sight, each of which, on an average, contained seven men, which is one thousand and fifty; and if we add half as many left on shore, and double that number for the women and children, the population of this group alone will amount to three thousand one hundred and fifty souls ... (Wilson 1799: 302).

Table 2 Total population, by sex, as reported by government and other sources, for Lamotrek Atoll, 1797–1971[1]

Year	Males	Females	Population	Sources and Remarks
1797	—	—	2000	Freycinet (Krämer 1937:10). This was the time of initial European contact. At least two severe typhoons struck the island between 1800 and 1890.
1890	—	—	300	Krämer 1937:10. This is probably an estimate made by the English trader Evan Lewis who was residing on the atoll.
1909	—	—	220	Krämer 1937:10. This estimate was made two years after the severe typhoon of 1907.
1920	—	—	93	Japanese Government.[2] There is some evidence that suggests a large number of residents had moved to Elato.
1925	—	—	204	Japanese Government.[3] An influenza epidemic swept through the area between 1925 and 1930.
1930	68	96	164	Japanese Government.[4]
1935	75	102	177	Japanese Government.[5] The events preceding and during World War II resulted in temporary displacement of some individuals and probably an increased incidence of veneral disease.
1948	—	—	152	Bryan 1970:17. Penicillin was introduced following World War II.
1955	76	84	160	U.S. State Dept., 1956[6]
1956	76	86	162	U.S. State Dept., 1957.
1957	78	88	166	U.S. State Dept., 1958. A moderate typhoon struck the island in 1957.
1958	83	89	172	U.S. State Dept., 1959.
1959	85	94	179	U.S. State Dept., 1960.
1960	85	93	178	U.S. State Dept., 1961.
1961	83	94	177	U.S. State Dept., 1962.
1962	99	102	201	This census was taken by the author in May 1962. Note the discrepancy with the following figure.

Table 2 (Continued)

Year	Males	Females	Population	Sources and Remarks
1962	90	94	184	U.S. State Dept., 1963.
1963	91	103	194	U.S. State Dept., 1964.
1964	88	101	189	U.S. State Dept., 1965.
1965	91	100	191	U.S. State Dept., 1966.
1966	91	100	191	U.S. State Dept., 1967.
1967	112	131	243	U.S. State Dept., 1968. This figure seems in error.
1968	96	102	198	U.S. State Dept., 1969.
1969	99	104	203	U.S. State Dept., 1970.
1970	103	112	215	U.S. State Dept., 1971.
1971	105	113	218	U.S. State Dept., 1972.

[1] All figures are *de facto* populations or thought to refer to *de facto* enumerations.

[2] This figure was obtained from a publication (Japan, Nanyo-cho 1931) reporting on the 1930 census of the Japanese Mandated Territories. Reference is made to earlier censuses of 1920 and 1925 which are not available to the author.

[3] Obtained from Japan, Nanyo-cho 1931.

[4] Japan, Nanyo-cho, 1931.

[5] Japan, Nanyo-cho, 1937.

[6] The U.S. State Department has provided census figures annually to the United Nations. The figures predating 1955 are not available to the author. The accuracy of these figures is suspect since few if any are based on controlled censuses. In general the enumerations refer to sometime between June and August of the enumeration year.

For this atoll that would have meant a density of 1800 persons per square mile (Table 3).

William Lessa (1962: 339–340) has cautioned that many early population estimates for the Caroline Islands were "obviously in error, especially in providing overestimates, but usually they are good approximations." As suggested by the two estimates cited here, it seems likely that the Lamotrek figure of Freycinet is such an overestimate. Even if we halve it, however, the population density for Lamotrek atoll was still a high 2638 persons per square mile—far greater than the 1200 per square mile of Java, traditionally considered one of the most densely settled agricultural regions of the world.

Wilson's reliability seems somewhat vindicated, however, by his estimate of 200 individuals on Ifaluk during the same voyage

Table 3 Total population, by sex, as reported by government and other sources, for Woleai Atoll, 1797–1971

Year	Males	Females	Population	Sources and Remarks
1797	—	—	3150	Wilson 1799:302. Made at the time of initial European contact. A severe typhoon struck the island about 1815.
1844	—	—	1500	Cheyne (Krämer 1937:195).
1862	—	—	600	Gulick (Krämer 1937:195).
1903	—	—	661	Krämer 1937:202. This is probably an estimate of the German physician Born.
1909	—	—	460	Krämer 1937:208–20. This is the first estimate available after the severe typhoon of 1907. Supposedly 180 Woleai typhoon refugees had moved to Elato.
1920	—	—	646	Japanese Government, 1931.[1]
1925	—	—	544	Japanese Government, 1931.
1930	235	303	538	Japanese Government, 1931.
1935	230	292	522	Japanese Government, 1937. There was great disruption and displacement caused by the events preceding and during World War II on this atoll. Among these was a probable increase in veneral disease.
1948	—	—	392	Bryan 1970:17. Penicillin was introduced at about this time.
1955	244	244	488	U.S. State Dept., 1956.
1956	242	241	483	U.S. State Dept., 1957.
1957	245	239	481	U.S. State Dept., 1958.
1958	244	244	488	U.S. State Dept., 1959.
1959	254	253	507	U.S. State Dept., 1960.
1960	254	253	507	U.S. State Dept., 1961.
1961	245	250	495	U.S. State Dept., 1962.
1962	246	254	500	U.S. State Dept., 1963.
1963	293	317	610	U.S. State Dept., 1964.
1964	277	274	551	U.S. State Dept., 1965.
1965	276	273	549	This census was taken by the author.
1965	265	265	530	U.S. State Dept., 1966.
1966	280	274	554	U.S. State Dept., 1967.
1967	319	325	644	U.S. State Dept., 1968.
1968	290	289	579	U.S. State Dept., 1969.
1969	299	287	586	U.S. State Dept., 1970.
1970	302	274	576	U.S. State Dept., 1971.
1971	297	282	576	U.S. State Dept., 1972.

[1] These figures are from the same sources as listed in Table 2.

of 1797. This figure does not appear to be an overestimate since the current population of this atoll is approximately 320 individuals. Later population figures for the two atolls of Woleai and Lamotrek provide the following picture:

WOLEAI. Andrew Cheyne, a British trader, visited the atoll in 1844 and estimated its population at 1500 individuals. In 1862, L. H. Gulick published a figure of 600, presumably determined after he visited the island. A German physician, named Born, who was working for the colonial administration of the time, visited the island twice, in 1903, when its population was 661, and in 1907 at the time of the severe typhoon mentioned in chapter 1, during which some 200 individuals were killed. If one deducts these deaths from the 1903 count, the resulting estimate of 460 seems quite close to a population figure derived from information provided by Augustin Krämer during his 1909 visit. Subsequent figures referring to the Japanese and American periods of administration are included in Table 3. All of these figures appear to be accurate estimates.

LAMOTREK. The literature for this atoll contains far fewer estimates. An English trader named Evan Lewis, who was resident on the island in 1880, gave a figure of 300. At the time Krämer visited the island in 1909 there were 220 residents. A Japanese census in 1927 listed 215, and one in 1930, following a severe influenza epidemic, lists 165 inhabitants. Subsequent Japanese and American figures are included in Table 2.

Nevertheless, based on present day techniques of horticulture and fishing and the estimates of productivity proposed earlier in the chapter, 1000 individuals does not seem an overestimate for the possible precontact population of Lamotrek. The single island of Lamotrek alone could support a population three times (or marginally four times) its present level. And it is known that in the past the two other islands of the atoll were also inhabited, probably adding two or three hundred additional individuals to the total population of the atoll. This easily reaches a figure of approximately 1000 individuals. Similarly, in the case of Woleai atoll it is estimated that Wottagai Island could have supported a population maximum of 400, Sùlywap 200, Falalus 300, and Falalap traditionally might have supported as many as 1400 individuals. In all, the whole atoll could reasonably support 2000 or more residents during periods of optimum productivity.

In precontact times, aside from warfare, the typhoon was probably the most significant variable affecting population numbers and productivity on these two atolls. The central Carolines lie in the typhoon belt of the western Pacific. In 1907 the typhoon which struck Woleai killed about 200, most of whom were swept from Raiur, the narrow island on the eastern side of the atoll. During the typhoons of more recent years, however, few deaths have been caused by drowning, wind-blown debris, falling trees or collapsing structures on these or neighboring atolls. A typhoon which hit Lamotrek in 1958 killed no one and the severe typhoon of 1960 on Ulithi only killed two individuals (Lessa 1964: 14). In both cases, though, agricultural production was significantly reduced on the atolls for some five to seven years. Thus if no aid were forthcoming, loss of life *after* a typhoon could be much greater than that suffered *during* the storm, owing to a subsequent and inevitable shortage of food.

Breadfruit trees are very susceptible to wind damage and are the first major crop to suffer in a typhoon. Cyrtosperma and other root crops are destroyed by salt water inundation and therefore are extensively affected on all but the smallest islets only by the most serious storms. The trend of growth and decline of population on Lamotrek and Woleai over a long period of time could periodically be influenced by destructive typhoons. Figure 4 is a graph depicting the population dynamics of the two atolls. It seems to substantiate this conclusion, at least with respect to the 1907 typhoon. If graphs could be constructed for precontact times they would probably show a similar trend, that is, periodic sharp decreases in population following a destructive typhoon, followed by a period of population growth as the island recovered its ability to support larger numbers of people, until a maximum was reached—if this point, in fact, was reached before another destructive typhoon struck the atoll. After a severe typhoon on Lamotrek, for example, the presumed 1000-person maximum could be halved as the result of direct and indirect typhoon-caused deaths. Assuming the population would subsequently grow at a rate of 1 percent per year, it would only take about 50 years for the population again to reach a near-maximum figure. Even this is a conservative

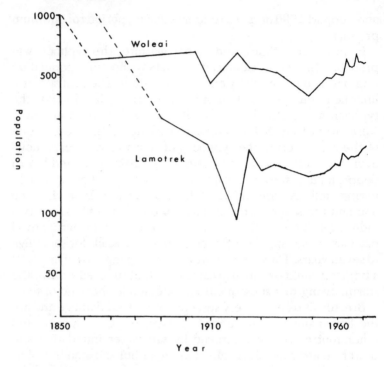

Figure 4 Woleai and Lamotrek population graph, 1850–1970.
(Population axis is plotted on semilog scale.)

estimate when viewed in the light of Tables 2 and 3 and the birth rate quoted earlier, which has the population of the area increasing some 3.5 percent per year.

William Lessa (1962: 340) reminds us that demographers have contended that island populations are very unstable, experiencing periodically rapid increase and just as rapid decline. Estimates of actual rates of increase and decline are, of course, not helped by inaccurate censuses, but the frequently erratic sequence of decline and growth seen in Tables 2 and 3 seems on the whole to confirm the demographers' hypotheses.

The rates of growth and decline on Woleai and Lamotrek are not exceptional, as one can note in comparing them to figures computed for Yap by Hunt, Kidder, and Schneider (1954). Yap is the closest volcanic island to Woleai and has experienced a somewhat similar history of contact. Its rates of population decline have been as great as 3 to 4 percent per annum during the period from 1900 to 1911. In the overall period from 1800 to 1950 on Lamotrek, a time of general postcontact population attrition, the average yearly decline was –1.70 percent (or –1.25 percent if 1000 is accepted as the initial population). From 1950 to 1972, a postpenicillin period of population increase, there was an average annual growth of +1.49 percent. For the same periods on Woleai, there was an annual overall loss of –1.38 percent between 1800 and 1950, and a rate of growth of +2.13 percent per year between 1950 and 1969. This latter figure could be somewhat inflated as the 1950 census may not have included all residents of the island, since some possibly had not yet returned to their homes from wartime exile on neighboring islands. By way of comparison, Ifaluk, which lies between Lamotrek and Woleai, had a population increase of +1.28 percent per year between 1950 and 1969, and Eauripik, the smallest inhabited atoll of the central Carolines, experienced an increase of +2.54 percent per year for the same period.

Undoubtedly there were, and are, a number of coral islands in Micronesia and Polynesia free from most factors of environmental stress, that have maintained their population numbers at a relatively constant level over a long period of time. On these islands the problems of population pressures on the carrying capacity of the island were obviously of continuous importance, and the adaptive strategies of these communities would continuously have to face problems that other communities only faced periodically.

The first settlers on the coral islands of Micronesia and Polynesia possessed a cultural inventory little different from that of a similar group of migrants making a landfall on one of the volcanic islands of these two regions. The inventory would not be identical in any two instances since it is highly unlikely that a canoe load of founders, whether arriving on a high or a low island would be completely representative of their home community. Nevertheless the basic cultural elements were drawn from a proto-Malayo-Polynesian cultural pool about which we can only speculate. Certainly the ancestral community possessed a marine and horticulturally oriented subsistence economic system. In addition it seems likely that it was also a culture within which ranking and status differentiation were important (Alkire 1977). Some analysts have suggested that social ranking in Malayo-Polynesian societies was originally tied to seniority of descent and membership in specific land holding groups, defined by bilateral kinship (Murdock 1948). Duality is also commonly found as an organizing principle in many spheres of the various societies and consequently is probably derived from this same Malayo-Polynesian antecedent culture. The social and economic structure was probably supported by belief in supernatural sanctions that were enforced by both ancestral and patron spirits who were guardians of kinsmen and occupational specialists. The institutional variations on these hypothesized antecedent forms are the result of differentiation following from isolation and adaptation.

The cultural background of migrants to high and low islands may have been similar, but the environments each confronted in their newly discovered islands were not. The coral island colonists were consistently faced with problems of adapting their technology and social system to a context of limited land where cultivation was often difficult owing to poor soils, frequent droughts and/or typhoons. In nearly every case the settlers were faced with an early realization that they had to maintain their population within a relatively narrow range of fluctuation, since community survival could be threatened both by underpopulation and overpopulation. The speed and frequency with which coral island communities were faced with population problems was far higher than that of volcanic island societies; hence perhaps more than any other single factor this has given most coral island societies a distinct similarity in contrast to their volcanic island neighbors.

Chapter 3

DAILY ACTIVITIES

It would be a mistake to assume, since most coral island communities are small, that day-to-day life is completely uneventful, routine, or dull. Tradition may determine the range of options acceptable for individual and community-wide decisions, but each day requires that specific choices be made. The general adaptive strategy retains a degree of flexibility in order to meet unusual combinations of environmental and social variables. This chapter will focus on the daily activities observed on Woleai atoll in the central Carolines over the period of a year, in order to illustrate this reality.

Woleai is a fairly typical atoll of its size and general characteristics within the central Caroline cultural region (Map 2). It is a medium-sized atoll of Micronesia, small when compared to Majuro or Kwajalein in the Marshalls, but large in comparison to Eauripik or Ifaluk, its nearest neighbors in the Carolines. The nearly 1.75 square miles of land area of Woleai is divided among a score of islands, seven of which are presently inhabited. The total resident population of the atoll has averaged between 500 and 600 individuals over the past 100 years. The settlement pattern on each of the islands is nearly identical. Dwellings are found lineally arranged along the lagoon side of an island, most often inland of the main path that runs the length of the island.

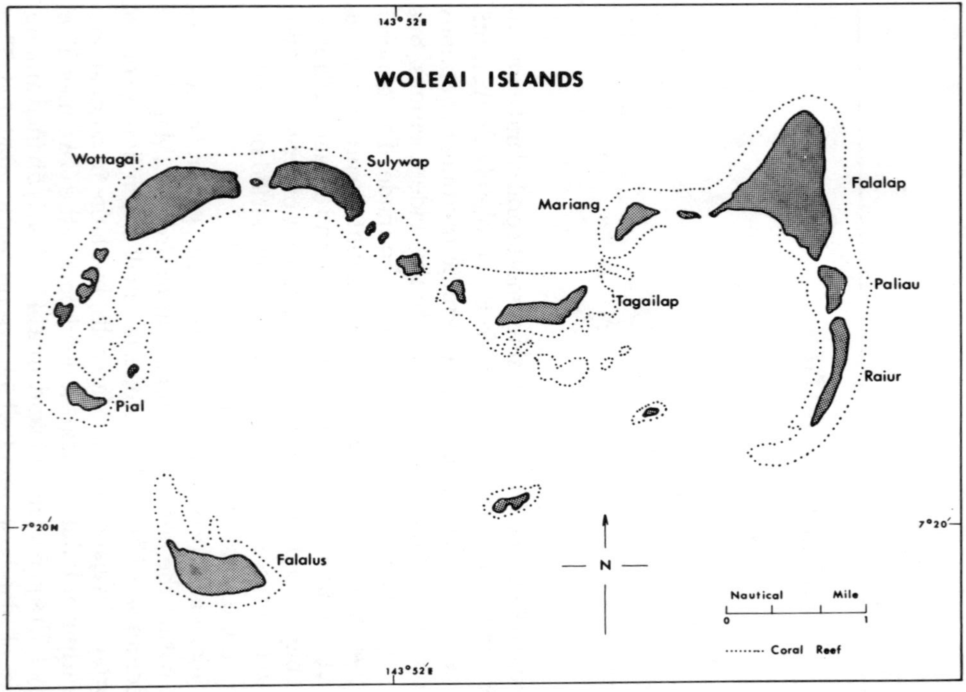

Map 2 Woleai Atoll

Each house is situated on a named plot and is either the seat of a matrilineage or closely affiliated with another dwelling that is.

Each dwelling houses a nuclear or extended family, including from three to fifteen or more individuals; the average house contains eight members and spans three or four generations. The floor plan of a dwelling is either rectangular or hexagonal. In a rectangular house the proportions are carefully controlled so that the width is always one-half the length of the structure. A hexagonal dwelling retains the same basic proportions, but, in addition, it has a small triangular alcove added to each end of the structure. All houses have steeply pitched thatched roofs with a considerable overhang at the eaves so that the roof reaches to within 3 feet of the ground. In more traditional times the status of occupants determined the pitch of the roof—a chief's house had a more steeply pitched roof than a commoner's, and a grave or spirit house had the most steeply pitched of all (Alkire 1970: 20).

Inside a dwelling one finds the simple arrangement of a single room, perhaps with the aforementioned small alcoves at each end. Logs, perhaps adzed into square beams, run along the ground between the corner posts. These form baseboards that serve to keep the gravel and mats on the earthen floor confined within the building. They also form the base of the walls which extend from the ground to the main plates and tie beams of the roof. The walls are usually plaited frond mats tied to a simple lattice work frame. Doors are placed at each end and perhaps on each side of the dwelling, thus providing entrance, ventilation, and light. All parts of the structure are either tied together with sennit twine or held in place by their own weight.

Finely plaited pandanus sleeping mats are unrolled for each occupant in the evening, but are generally stored against the walls or overhead in the rafters during the day. At one end of the structure may be a small hearth, although most cooking is usually done in a separate structure, a cooking house, removed from the dwelling. This serves not only to reduce the risk of fire in the dwelling, but also keeps to a minimum the number of rats that are attracted by food to the dwelling. Against one of the walls or in an alcove the woman or women of the house will have afixed one or more backstrap looms, used for weaving loincloths and skirts. At various places along the walls storage

boxes and trunks are placed which contain the personal posses-
sions of household members. The most valuable household
effects are carefully wrapped and stored overhead in the rafters
of the structure, relatively safe from curious children and cove-
tous relatives. Mosquito nets and a cradle may also hang overhead, strung from the rafters so that they can easily be lowered
when needed. Most houses contain very little beyond these
basic items; little more is really needed since the dwelling is
primarily a sleeping area for the family and secondarily a work
area for women when they are weaving. Otherwise it is vacated
by its occupants during the day.

The yard around the dwelling is also covered with fine coral
gravel and periodically is cleaned of fallen leaves and twigs by
the children and old women of the household. The cooking
house stands removed 10 or more yards from the dwelling and
one or more open racks, raised about 3 feet from the ground,
are situated nearby where pots and containers are placed out
of the reach of wandering dogs. These racks are also used for
smoking fish whenever a large catch is made. At such times the
pots and pans are removed and a small fire is built below the
rack. In some cases a small menstrual house is also found on
individual homesteads, removed from the dwelling, but in
other cases the women of the lineage use a communal menstrual house usually located near the beach at one end of the
island.

The chickens that belong to the household wander about
freely, roosting in trees or on roofs at night. Pigs are tied by a
foreleg to trees or penned in log structures usually removed to
some more distant part of the homestead lands. Dogs are the
only other domestic animals, and they wander at will.

In each village or district of an island there is one or more
canoe house, usually at least one for each landholding clan of
that district. The canoe houses also line the main path of the
island, but are most often opposite the dwellings on the lagoon
side of the path near the water. Other public structures are
spaced throughout the village. In recent years these include a
communal store, a small primary school, a dispensary, a church,
and perhaps a copra drying kiln. All of these modern structures
were, until very recent years, built of traditional materials.

In 1965 this was the general setting of Woleai life, a life that was still essentially adapted to subsistence horticulture and fishing and consequently little changed from that of the previous 100 years. Horticulture emphasized Cyrtosperma and breadfruit cultivation, and fishing concentrated on reef and nearby open ocean exploitation. Early each day women from various households proceeded to the taro swamps to weed, mulch, and harvest, returning with a basketful of Cyrtosperma or Colocasia later in the morning. The rest of their day was spent either preparing food, gathering other foods such as breadfruit or coconuts, weaving, cleaning, and tending to other domestic chores. Similarly, early each morning the men of a household first set out to tap their coconut trees for *falubwa* (sweet toddy) or *hachi* (palm wine). Thereafter the men proceeded to a canoe house where individually or collectively they would either set out to fish for the morning or engage in some type of fishing related labor—repairing or manufacturing canoes, nets, spears, or traps. In the course of a day both sexes had ample opportunity to sit and chat in their respective work areas with friends and relatives. In all, each sex devoted some 4 to 6 hours of each day to concentrated work. All residents of a homestead usually returned to their dwelling late in the afternoon when the main meal of the day was taken. A light morning meal was generally consumed before setting off to work. This was supplemented by light snacks of coconuts or other tidbits of available food wherever one happened to be working.

Probably the ebb and flow of daily life and the progression of yearly events can best be conveyed by presenting appropriate extracts from the activity diary the author kept while on the atoll in 1965.

JANUARY 29, 1965. The M/V Errol arrived at Wottagai Island, Woleai at noon today and I off-loaded my equipment. At a meeting arranged by the field trip officer, the chief of Tabwogap district, Igeilimai, suggested I take up residence in his district in the island dispensary, which has been unmanned and vacant since the death of the island health aid several months ago. The next 3 days were spent in establishing camp.

FEBRUARY 1. Igeilimai asked me to attend a general meeting of the men of the island held this morning at Fasafang canoe house in Pigùl district (Map 3). When we arrived most of the other men had assembled and were seated within and in

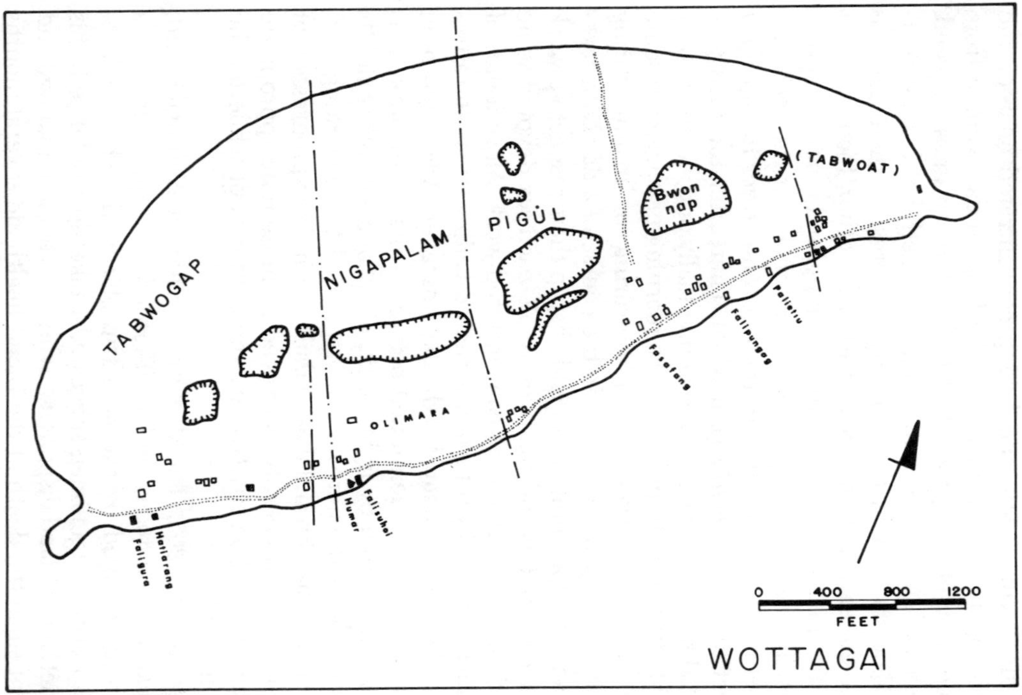

Map 3 Wottagai Island

front of the structure. The focus of the discussion concerned the numbers of *cho* (mature coconuts) that were to be contributed by each estate *(bwogot)* in a funeral exchange with Falalus Island. Several of the older men made suggestions, and it was finally decided that it might be best to send a canoe to Falalus in order to consult with that island's chief on his intended contribution to this exchange.

FEBRUARY 2. This morning Igeilimai told me that a large catch of bonito *(harangap)* had been taken near Falalap Island yesterday evening and that Wottagai would receive a portion of the catch later in the day. At 9:05 A.M. three men, including one of the chiefs of Falalap, arrived by canoe at Faligura canoe house (Tabwogap district), bringing bonito. Apparently the catch was exceptionally large, one small canoe had returned with 120 fish, while scores of other fish had been left on the beach of Paliau Island for lack of transport until such time as other canoes could be dispatched from Falalap to pick them up. In all the catch must have totaled several hundred fish. The Wottagai share was distributed among all the estates of the island, and the portions that could not be consumed immediately were smoked by the various recipients and stored.

FEBRUARY 3. The men who were to travel to Falalus for consultation about the funeral exchange had to postpone their voyage for a day because of the bonito catch. This coconut exchange apparently will end the prolonged funeral ceremonies that followed the deaths of nine people during an influenza epidemic of last summer. This exchange is one that quite accurately can be termed symbolic. The chiefs have decided to exchange 2000 nuts. Falalus will "receive" the Wottagai nuts and Wottagai will receive those gathered on Falalus, but neither assemblage is actually removed from its island of origin. Rather, the nuts gathered on each island are redistributed as though they have been received from the other island. According to an informant, Falalus and Wottagai do this "because we are *one* people."

FEBRUARY 7. Two canoes arrived from Falalus and Falalap bringing chiefs from each of these islands for a meeting at Fasafang canoe house with the chiefs and senior men of Wottagai and Sùlywap. The discussion concerned the high school students from Woleai who are attending school on Ulithi. The principal of the Ulithi school sent a letter via the M/V Errol to the chiefs of Woleai saying he wanted the students to remain at Ulithi through the summer. After some discussion the chiefs decided they would inform the principal that they preferred the students to return here for the summer because (1) they needed these boys to help in cleaning up the islands from the effects of a tropical storm of several weeks ago; (2) they should have an opportunity to visit with relatives after being away for so long; (3) the local teachers will in any case be going to Ulithi for the summer so the atoll will be short of manpower as it is; and (4) they feared Ulithi would not have enough food to support so many temporary residents for such a long period of time.

A second item of discussion concerned a dance these same students participated in on Ulithi. The chiefs of Woleai did not approve of the activity because "our customs do not permit us to wear red cloth on Yap or Ulithi or dance on those islands." The chiefs decided to talk with the field trip officer about the problem on his next visit and possibly to send an emmisary to Ulithi.

FEBRUARY 10. A canoe arrived at Wottagai from Falalap bringing several young men to pick up coconuts and taro that are being sent to Falalap in exchange for the bonito Wottagai recently received from that island.

FEBRUARY 22. The field trip ship unexpectedly arrived at the atoll this morning, and the men of the atoll are busily sacking and carrying copra to the beach for sale. Sales and purchases on all seven islands of the atoll were completed by February 24 when the ship departed for Olimarao and the Lamotrek area.

MARCH 4. This morning while gathering information on various chants from Marial and Fagoisap these two men told me about the *galigi* ceremony (Alkire 1968). This was a ceremony that formerly took place shortly after a porpoise catch. It had as its primary objective the performance of magic meant to increase taro yields. The ceremony suggests some interesting conceptual relationships between porpoises (from the sea), taro (from the land), male activities (fishing), and female activities (gardening).

MARCH 7. Igeilimai sailed to Falalap this morning in order to visit a Ulithi woman who arrived on the M/V Errol several days ago. This woman is a classificatory daughter to Igeilimai who himself once lived on Ulithi while married to a Ulithian. Teomal and another man went spear fishing this morning in order to obtain fish to give to a woman of Sùlywap who gave birth two days ago.

MARCH 13. Shalif, the man who is *holas* (assistant) to Igeilimai, went through Tabwogap and Nigapalam districts today tying *ubwut* (immature coconut fronds) to palms along the main path at intervals of approximately 100 yards. These signify a *sapet* which is part of the funeral ceremony for the nine people who died during last summer's epidemic. For the duration of the *sapet* the trees of the districts cannot have nuts taken from them and no copra can be made of nuts within the districts for three or more months.

MARCH 16. I have been taking a census of Sùlywap island for the last two days. Most of the people of Sùlywap are making copra. Yagamai, one of the senior men of the island, said that he intended to impose a *sapet* here this evening for the same reason one was invoked on Wottagai three days ago. Apparently there are two kinds of *sapet*, one large and one small. The latter follows the former after several months and the current one appears to be the second one imposed for these particular deaths.

MARCH 22. Most of the men of Wottagai sailed to Sùlywap in three canoes this morning. They are going to contribute labor to the repair of a canoe house on that island, which needs new roof braces, rafters, and thatch. The canoe house was originally built in 1946. In all, 34 men and 10 boys are involved in the work. Two of the men came from Falalap in a paddling canoe. All of the workers are fed by Sùlywap women at completion of the day's work.

MARCH 23. The Wottagai men again travelled to Sùlywap to complete work on the canoe house. The two men of Falalap also returned bringing 500 fathoms of coconut sennit twine as a contribution to the work. According to an informant certain lineages of Ifang district on Falalap always contribute to events such as this on Sùlywap because "they had the same *sawei* on

Yap." (See chapter 6 for a discussion of the *sawei* exchange system.)

MARCH 24. Erur sailed to Falalap this morning with several baskets of taro intended for kinsmen on that island who are building a canoe. Apparently Falalap has more timber available for canoe construction than any other island of the atoll.

MARCH 27. Several women from Pigül district and Sülywap came to Tabwogap to clean the area of weeds around the community store. This is the only store for the two islands and the residents of the various districts alternate in this kind of labor. This evening after observing the moon Igeilimai mentioned that tomorrow is the anniversary of the 1907 typhoon which destroyed the community on Raiur Island. (According to Krämer some 200 people of Woleai were killed during the typhoon of March 29 and 30, 1907.)

MARCH 29. I sailed to Falalus this morning in order to observe the *tairang* (puberty) ceremony of a young girl. This girl had informed her mother that her menses had started on the 28th. The *tairang* or *legot* ceremony conducted by Letauopi, a senior woman, began on the 29th. Letauopi recited the necessary chants and snapped two *ubwut* (frond pinnae) that had been knotted in a special way, while both were seated facing each other. For four days during the ceremony the young girl is permitted to wear a woven skirt *(tur)* for the first time. After six days the chant is repeated but the girl will not wear a *tur* on this occasion. She is required to remain near the menstrual house and is specifically prohibited from entering any taro swamp. She is expected to bathe frequently in the lagoon near the menstrual house and when she walks to the water she shields herself with a frond mat from the view of any men who may be working or lounging in a nearby canoe house up the beach. She is always accompanied to the water by a large number of young children, both boys and girls, who swarm around her as she walks to her bath. A small hut will be constructed for her near the menstrual house where she will take up residence and remain until she again returns to the menstrual house next month. She remains here for five menstruations—usually something over four months—and after that period she is permitted to wear a *tur* as her adult dress and return to her normal dwelling.

Each evening for the first four days of the *tairang* all of the adult men and women of Falalus assemble to dance. The dances are called *kasig* or *huluhul* and include chants of praise and "false praise." The first extol the outstanding characteristics, often with sexual references, of individuals on neighboring islands. The chants of "false praise" similarly refer to the superiority of neighbors, but in this case individuals who are known to be handicapped in one or another way—senile, physically unattractive, crippled, and so on. All participants are highly amused by the latter references. These dances and chants, unlike others performed at night, are always done in darkness, without nearby fires, in order that male and female performers in opposite ranks will not be embarrased by the performance of a relative in the other group.

APRIL 3. After returning to Wottagai Island I noted that two canoes belonging to Olifeimag estate and housed in Falipungag canoe house had coconut frond taboo signs *(mushang)* tied to their prows. Apparently one of the chiefs of Falalap discovered that a young man with patrilateral ties to Olifeimag, who is married to one of his classificatory daughters, committed adultery with another married woman. If the Olifeimag lineage does not pay compensation *(haria)* in the form of 10 to 20 woven skirts, loincloths, and cloth, the offended chief will confiscate the two canoes. Compensation will also have to be given to the offended husband.

APRIL 13. While working on genealogies this morning I heard a radio report locating a typhoon north of Pikelot. Later in the afternoon I saw Hatiomai seated near the beach in front of Faligura canoe house engaged in knot divination *(bwe)*. He was chanting while taking two different readings to determine if the typhoon was going to strike the atoll (Alkire 1970: 13–16). When he finished he gave the knotted pinnae to his young son who placed them beneath a coconut palm on the west side of the canoe house where all *bwe* leaves of the canoe house group are deposited.

APRIL 14. The wind is now from the south and the barometer rising. Last night the discussion of the men at Faligura naturally centered on typhoons, and Igeilimai demonstrated an exceptionally accurate memory regarding the 1907 typhoon. He recalled that a German ship had been in the lagoon at the time and that two German "company" men and one doctor had been ashore on Falalap and Mariang islands when the storm struck. The ship was driven from the lagoon and returned several days later bringing relief food. All of the islands of the atoll were severely damaged, so the ship took between 160 and 180 people as refugees to Saipan and Elato, most of them from Falalap and Falalus islands. Only one Wottagai man joined the group. Many of these people returned to Woleai during Japanese times, but others either died there or chose to remain on Saipan. Later in the evening I reread Krämer's account of the typhoon and it supported Igeilimai's description almost point-for-point.

Earlier in the day two men arrived from Falalus and mentioned that Malush, the chief of Falalus, told everyone yesterday to secure their houses since a typhoon was nearby. There is no radio on Falalus and no one from here travelled there yesterday. Several men commented on the accuracy of Malush's weather forecasting ability.

APRIL 29. I sailed to Paliau this morning to work on a census of the island. A Satawal canoe arrived at Falalap yesterday. The canoe originally departed Satawal for Lamotrek and Elato. When it arrived at Elato the Satawal voyagers found that a man on that island wished to return to Woleai, so they volunteered to transport him. Rupungalap and Rupungalug, the two brothers in charge of the canoe, and the five other men left Elato at 7:30 A.M. on the 27th; they sighted Ifaluk at 7:30 on the 28th, but bypassed this island and continued on to Falalap where they arrived at 3:30 P.M. The canoe thus averaged a speed of 4 knots for the trip.

MAY 4. I accompanied three canoes that sailed from Wottagai to Falalus this morning, transporting several baskets of food and bottles of *hachi* (palm wine) as gifts for the Satawal men who have since moved to Falalus. On our return from Falalus we received seven pots of breadfruit and several dozen coconuts from the Satawalese as return gifts; these were assembled from among the food that they had received from relatives and friends on Falalus.

MAY 5. From Wottagai I saw the Satawal canoe leave Falalus about 11:30 A.M. and later observed it leaving the atoll through the east channel about 5:00 P.M., apparently on its way back to Satawal.

MAY 11. A canoe from Falalap arrived at Tabwogap this afternoon with three emissaries sent to inform this island of a *shufelu* gathering of the islands on Falalap tomorrow. The purpose of the *shufelu* is to terminate the funeral ceremonies of Olalegai, the former chief of Ifang district and to witness the installation of a new chief for that district.

MAY 12. This morning three canoes from Tabwogap, three from Pigul, five from Falalus, and four from Sûlywap set sail for Falalap carrying most of the adult men, but no women of these islands, to the Falalap *shufelu*. I noted two canoes across the lagoon from Tagailap also proceeding directly to Falalap. When our canoe arrived in the east lagoon we hove-to off Raiur and waited for all of the other canoes of the western islands to arrive. We then set sail again as a compact fleet, with the canoes carrying the chiefs of Sûlywap, Wottagai, and Falalus leading the way. All steered for Faliangiang canoe house of Ifang district.

After landing all of the visitors assembled in the canoe house and awaited developments. Arranged nearby were several large piles of drinking nuts, ripe coconuts, and baskets of food. The chancellor *(holas)* of Ifang district then addressed the group saying there were 20 bunches of drinking coconuts and 40 baskets of food in the piles donated by the chiefs of this island and 40 bunches of nuts and 40 additional baskets of food donated by the other men of the island. He went on to say that there were *cho* coconuts assembled to be distributed as follows: 1000 for Tabwogap, 1000 for Nigapalam, 1000 for Pigûl, 1000 for Sûlywap, and 1000 for Falalus. One thousand in these cases meant 100 bunches *(iaf)*, each of which contained 8 nuts, or an actual total of 800 nuts for each island (Alkire 1970: 10–13). He also called out allotments for representatives of "greater" Lamotrek (meaning Lamotrek, Elato, and Satawal), Mogmog, Faraulep, Eauripik, Fais, and Ifaluk. These were collected by local residents who had close kin ties with the appropriate island, since those islands, of course, were not able to send actual delegates.

After the distribution one of the chiefs of Sûlywap addressed the assembly with a complaint. He felt that notice of the *shufelu* was too short and unexpected. He said that previously the chiefs of Falalap had said they would not have a *shufelu,* but then yesterday the canoe had arrived to inform him of it. Consequently, the western islands had no time to prepare food or nuts to contribute as they normally would be expected to do. Igeilimai supported these comments and added that the *shufelu* was a celebration for chiefs and thus the chiefs rightfully should have been notified in advance. One of the Falalap chiefs responded by saying that he knew that on most islands the chiefs came first, but here on Falalap the people came first followed by the chiefs. This comment only provoked Igeilimai to elaborate on the procedural errors committed by the organizers of this *shufelu.*

The Ifang chancellor turned the conversation to the appointment of a new chief for the district. Igeilimai said it must be the eldest man of the proper lineage and he pointed out whom he meant. All of the other chiefs agreed that this was the proper choice. The man designated acknowledged the appointment, saying he would accept only if the people supported his decisions. He stated he would not take up the position if they intended to disobey him. This appeared to be the normal response on such occasions. These speeches completed the formal parts of the ceremony, and the men then settled back to drink palm wine and await the dances that the women of the host island customarily perform for the *shufelu.* The visitors were soon informed, however, that there would be no dancing since the usual dances, which traditionally included erotic and suggestive overtones, were thought out of keeping for the now-Christian community. This took the visitors by surprise, which turned to keen disappointment, when they also found that there were only three or four cups of palm wine per man provided by the hosts. Shortly thereafter, then, the visitors from the western islands loaded their canoes with the allotments of coconuts and baskets of food and set sail for home. For the full 5 miles across the lagoon my companions compared this *shufelu* unfavorably with those of the "golden" past.

MAY 29. Hatiomai sent a Calophyllum *(ragash)* log from Wottagai to Falalus today. The log was given to him by his wife and taken from her lands. He is sending it to his own lineage on

Falalus as his contribution to the construction of a medium-sized sailing canoe. This hardwood log will be used for the keel section of the hull.

JUNE 6. Breadfruit is now being picked on a regular basis. The trees began bearing in May and will continue to provide fruit until September. A small number of trees even bear into October or November. The women ask particular men (their husbands, brothers, or sons) to climb the trees in order to pick the fruit with long bamboo poles. The bamboo is imported from Yap or Truk since none grows on the atoll. The women stand below the trees and catch or retrieve the fruit which they place in baskets and carry back to their cook house. During the height of the harvest season, quantities of surplus breadfruit are preserved by the women. They first soak the fruit in the lagoon overnight, then carry it to an area near the cooking house of their estate. There they peel and mash it. The mashed fruit is then placed in holes that have been excavated nearby. The holes are lined with leaves and when full are covered with frond mats that are held in place by piles of coral stones. The fruit preserved in this way is called *mar* and will keep for up to two years, although it must be removed every few months in order to renew the lining of leaves. When it is taken out for consumption a portion is wrapped in leaves and either steamed, baked in ground ovens, or roasted on hot coals before eating.

JUNE 29. The M/V Errol arrived this morning bringing the high school students back from Ulithi for the summer. I boarded the ship for a visit to the eastern islands of Faraulep, Satawal, Lamotrek, Elato, and Ifaluk and returned with the ship to Woleai on July 9.

JULY 28. I moved my base camp from Wottagai across the lagoon to Falalus today.

JULY 31. Several men paddled out in canoes in an attempt to surround and trap a school of fish near the shore of Falalus. This is only one of several times that I have observed this kind of activity and usually the school swims off before they reach the area. This type of fishing did not occur on Wottagai and probably takes place here because of the particular reef configuration near Falalus.

AUGUST 2. This afternoon at about 5:00 P.M. a *shúwar* moving ceremony was performed. The *shúwar* ceremony is meant to purify a woman who has recently given birth before she is permitted to leave the birth house and return to her usual dwelling. The shaman in charge prepared eight *chùlim* for the ceremony. A *chùlim* consists of two mountain apple leaves tied with coconut frond pinnae *(ubwut)*. The shaman prepared these near Falumai canoe house and after they were all tied he chanted to the six spirits of the *shùwar.* He then gave the eight *chùlim* to another man, who was related to the woman preparing to leave the birth house, and the latter carried the leaves to an area near the birth house where he dropped them on the ground before he returned to the canoe house. Shortly afterwards the woman, who gave birth on March 30th, with her baby and several women attendants emerged from the house and picked up the *chùlim.* The mother placed one in the baby basket, one in her belt behind, and carried one. The others were divided among her attendants. The group then left the area and walked in file to the woman's residence where other members of her family awaited the arrival of the group.

AUGUST 5. A small school of bonito was seen in the reef pocket at the west end of Falalus this morning. Several men took a large encircling net from one of the canoe houses to the area on a medium-sized paddling canoe. Most of the other able-bodied men, women, and children of the island proceeded to the area by foot along the beach or in small one-man paddling canoes. The net was set around the outside of the school and ropes attached at each end were led ashore. All of the villagers then situated themselves along the rope and net at intervals of about 10 feet out into the lagoon. The women and children were close in-shore and the younger men farther out into the lagoon where they had to swim and tread water. At the direction of two or three of the older men, who were acting as master fishermen, everyone began to pull the net by means of the ropes towards the shore from both ends. The net and its catch were beached after some 30 to 45 minutes of this work. In this case only 20 bonito were caught and these were distributed equally among all estates of the island.

AUGUST 7. Wolemel arrived on Falalus this morning from Pigùl district, Wottagai. He brought some freshly butchered pork as a gift for one of the young boys of Falalus who will soon be returning to school on Ulithi.

This evening a signal fire was seen across the lagoon on Falalap Island. This was interpreted as a sign that someone on that island was gravely ill or had died. A canoe departed Falalus for Falalap to investigate the matter at 9:00 P.M. These men took several woven skirts and loincloths with them as funeral gifts *(tugatug)* in case their interpretation was correct.

AUGUST 10. I accompanied most of the men of the village *rop* fishing this morning. *Rop* fishing is a netting technique that uses a somewhat smaller surround net in the lagoon along the reef. In this case the lead ropes attached to the shorter sennit net have coconut frond pinnae attached to them so that these pinnae hang down into the water simulating a continuous barrier. The fish swim away from the fronds and thus are gradually encircled by the net itself. While in the lagoon we saw a signal mirror flashing on Falalap, which was soon answered by flashes from Falalus. When we returned to Falalus from the reef another canoe was dispatched to Falalap to investigate.

AUGUST 11. One of the canoes returned from Falalap this afternoon and informed us that Taiwei had died on that island.

This evening a small party was held in one of the canoe houses to celebrate the completion of construction on Saiel's new canoe. The moon was full this evening so many of the young boys went *ragum* (terrestrial crab) hunting along the main path and near the taro swamps. The women have been gathering at the menstrual house for the last two nights and practicing dancing.

AUGUST 16. A canoe arrived from Pigùl this morning bringing 100 taro corms as *hophopilifal,* that is, a food distribution made in honor of a recently deceased man (in this case one of the men who died during last summer's epidemic) on the first occasion following his death when a canoe house he frequented is rethatched. In this instance Fasafang canoe house on Wottagai was rethatched several days ago. In addition to the 100 corms distributed here, two days ago 300 were taken to Falalap and 600 others were distributed on Wottagai and Sùlywap. In all 1000 tubers were distributed for this *hophopilifal.*

AUGUST 17. Men again are preparing copra in anticipation of the trading ship's arrival. Several men are also engaged in carving canoe paddles at one of the canoe houses.

AUGUST 20. I noted that several of the women were harvesting larger than usual amounts of taro this morning. Baskets of the food are being prepared to send to Sûlywap for a woman who recently gave birth. There are six kinds of labor women perform in the taro fields: (1) Excavation *(bwúlikúl)* is necessary if no natural depression exists. Both men and women may be involved in this labor, but it is not common on Woleai as many natural swamps are found here. This work is common on Eauripik. (2) Mulching *(walnibwúl)* involves placing of humus in the area to be planted. (3) Planting *(fät)* involves setting out seed corms in newly prepared areas. (4) Weeding *(feifei)* around the plants is frequent. (5) Grubbing may also be necessary if the plot is small. It involves working around the circumference of the area cutting out all roots of other plants and trees that are found growing into the plot from neighboring areas. (6) Harvesting is referred to by two terms. *Wugúlibwúl* is the term used for harvesting Cyrtosperma *(bwulog)*. In traditional times it was only permissible to do this before sunrise. The actual procedure involved cutting the tuber loose with a digging stick, after which the base of the stem was cut away from the tuber and replanted with the leaves trimmed away. The remaining part of the tuber was placed in a harvest basket. *Húlihúli* is a term that refers to the digging up and harvesting of Colocasia *(uot)*. This is generally executed with greater care than *wugúlibwúl* and actually involves digging the earth away from around the plant.

AUGUST 21. A canoe left with eight baskets of taro for the woman on Sûlywap, but it had to turn back because of a squall. The men set out again about 4:30 P.M. and successfully completed the trip.

AUGUST 22. Two canoes sailed to Wottagai this morning for a chiefs' meeting. The chiefs of Wottagai, Falalus, and Sûlywap discussed an exchange of coconuts which will end the funeral ceremonies for an old woman who died earlier in the year.

AUGUST 25. The Wottagai/Sûlywap–Falalus ceremonial funeral exchange discussed on the 22nd "occurred" today. The nuts that had been assembled on Falalus were now the nuts sent by Wottagai/Sûlywap and consequently they were redistributed equally to the ten estates of Falalus. The total distributed on this occasion was 1529 bunches of 10 (each of which actually contained 8 as discussed previously). Each estate received 100 bunches (800 nuts). There remained 529 bunches to distribute and these were given to the households on the island that had contributed *tugatug* (funeral offerings) at the time of the old woman's death. A similar distribution of nuts on Wottagai and Sùlywap took place, with the nuts "given" to those islands by Falalus.

AUGUST 30. The women held a dance this afternoon to honor the high school students who will soon be leaving for Ulithi. The dancing began at 3:00 P.M. with single-line standing dances, followed by double-line standing dances, and ending with single-line sitting dances. The performance was completed at 5:00 P.M.

SEPTEMBER 3. Most of the men sailed in five canoes to a section of the reef near Tagailap Island for fishing this morning. This is the reef section that Falalus shares rights in with Iur district, Falalap. The community fishing is in preparation for a party to be held for the departing high school students. A turtle was also caught at the west end of Falalus this morning.

SEPTEMBER 4. The men went fishing again today and the turtle caught yesterday was butchered and distributed in preparation for the party tomorrow. Each estate of the island is contributing fourteen drinking coconuts, two baskets of taro or breadfruit, and two bottles of palm wine to the party. Yarofailig took a share of the turtle to Wottagai this afternoon. Such shares are given to the chiefs of that island even if only one turtle is caught.

SEPTEMBER 5. Three canoes each from Wottagai and Sùlywap and one from Falalap arrived for the party. The food gathered was distributed by household at 10:00 A.M. The women danced while the men sat in and around the canoe house drinking palm wine. During the dancing individual men offerred gifts of tobacco, matches, and pilot biscuits over the heads of favorite dancers. The festivities continued until 3:00 P.M. when the visiting canoes departed for their home islands.

SEPTEMBER 7. Work began today on rethatching Falimai canoe house. This afternoon a small catch of bonito was made by surround net at the west end of the island.

SEPTEMBER 8. This morning the men went into the interior and to the oceanside of the island gathering coconut fronds.

These were brought to the area beside Falimai where the women had assembled to plait them into thatch sheets. The thatching was completed by this afternoon.

SEPTEMBER 19. The field trip ship arrived this morning to buy copra and pick up school students for transport to Ulithi. Three boys from Falalus will be attending this year.

SEPTEMBER 23. I travelled with the chiefs of Falalus to a meeting (*tei*) at Nigapalam canoe house on Wottagai. The meeting was to discuss sending a representative to Yap, as requested by the field trip officer during his visit in preparation for the outer islands joining the Yap District Congress. There was prolonged discussion about the advantages and disadvantages of joining this body (cf. Meller 1969).

SEPTEMBER 26. This morning Saiel, Malush, and Sepel seated themselves beside the navigators' *(pelu)* trees near Halingafang canoe house for the purpose of knot divination *(bwe)*. They undertook this in order to determine who should represent Falalus at the chiefs' meeting on Yap regarding the Yap District Congress. Saiel was ultimately chosen as the island's delegate.

OCTOBER 12. This evening a large number of bonito was caught by the usual surround net technique at the west end of the island. The catch numbered more than 175 fish. After a hundred or more of the fish had been thrown ashore, enough to provide shares for all households, the old men in charge of the fishing told the women that they could have the rest. This was a signal for all of the women who had participated in pulling the net to shore to leave their positions and jump into the shallow water containing the remaining fish encircled by the net. The women set about grabbing as many fish as possible and throwing them to designated companions on the beach. The scene became one of near pandemonium with various women grabbing at thrashing fish while the men called out in wild amusement. This event is a departure from the usual equal distribution of fish among all households, since each woman gets to keep all of the fish she personally takes for her own household or estate. Several *fafa* (rainbow runners) were also taken in the net and these were set aside for the women of the menstrual house, who are not permitted to eat bonito.

OCTOBER 22. Today was designated path cleaning day by the chiefs. The men started at the east end of the main path and the women at the west end and the two groups began working towards the mid-point of the island.

OCTOBER 25. The path cleaning was completed today. The women reached the mid-point before the men so the men were obliged to present gifts of drinking coconuts to the women. The women were seated at the mid-point chatting and smoking when the men finally completed their work and they liberally offered hoots and chants commenting on how slow and lazy the men were. The men retired, somewhat embarrassed, to return with their gift coconuts.

NOVEMBER 4. A signal fire was sighted on Wottagai early this morning indicating a death on that island. I joined the canoes that set off for Wottagai later in the morning. When we arrived we discovered that Legaretip, the senior woman of Saufalachig clan, had died. Two canoes also arrived from Falalap. The body was laid out in one of the canoe houses and many of the women of the island were seated around it singing dirges and wailing. Igeilimai, Tiamaral, and Maileg, all of the same clan as the deceased, were seated at one side of the canoe house receiving *tugatug* funeral offerings from the various individuals as they arrived. Tiamaral noted each gift in a small account book. A coffin was being built from an old paddling canoe a few yards away by a number of men. The body was wrapped in numerous *tur* and when the coffin was finished it too was lined with more woven skirts and several mosquito nets and blankets. The body was placed in the coffin and the lid firmly tied on. Two of the senior women from the same household as the deceased rubbed the coffin with turmeric *(rang)*. Shortly thereafter it was carried to the graveyard with the mourners following in procession. After burial most of the close relatives who cared for the dead woman when she was ill returned to the canoe house where they will continue to live and sleep for several days. They will be supplied with food by the other villagers.

NOVEMBER 12. Igeilimai sent a canoe to Falalus to fetch me for a *hubwulimäs* party for the dead given as part of the funeral ceremony for the recently deceased old woman of his clan. Several baskets of taro, rice, pork, turtle, and fish were all distributed at this event.

DECEMBER 1. Bwemo asked me if I could provide some medicine for the girl whose puberty ceremony was held eight months ago (March 28). The girl has been complaining of abdominal pains and has not menstruated for two months; from the time she saw a *yalus* (ghost) in the doorway of her house. She is about 11 years old.

DECEMBER 6. I observed *ulaam* trap fishing on the reef at the west end of the island today. Two canoes from Iur, Falalap brought some bonito to Falalus as *igalifelu* "fish of the island" shares. These were sent because of the intra-atoll *(chúlifeimag)* ties Iur has with Falalus (discussed in chapter 6).

DECEMBER 21. A going-away party was held for me this afternoon since I will return to Wottagai tomorrow. Fifteen bunches of drinking nuts were distributed, ten pots of food, several chickens, bonito, canned fish, and palm wine were provided. I was also given two tur that had been woven by all of the women of the island. In return I distributed gifts to all of the estates of the island.

DECEMBER 22. I moved back to Wottagai this morning in order to finish some work here before leaving on the ship early next month.

DECEMBER 31. All of the men of Wottagai and Sùlywap proceeded to the east end of Sùlywap where a school of mullet had been sighted. The school was trapped in a surround net and the total catch numbered 320 fish. These were distributed so that each resident of the two islands received one and a half fish.

JANUARY 1, 1966. The chiefs of Wottagai and Sùlywap intended to have an all-residents meeting and party at Fasafang canoe house in order to discuss the events of the past year and future plans, but heavy rain this morning prevented many Sùlywap people from coming. The Wottagai residents did attend and afterwards F., who had consumed a great deal of palm wine, later fell from a coconut palm he had climbed to tap. Igeilimai proceeded to the injured man's house to treat him after being called by the man's relatives. Igeilimai diagnosed that the man had a broken leg and possible rib fractures and then proceeded to set the bones by traditional massage techniques. He also massaged the man's abdomen as a precaution against internal injuries.

JANUARY 2. Igeilimai returned to Pigùl early this morning in order to continue treatment of F.

JANUARY 7. The trading ship entered the lagoon early this morning and anchored near Falalus. I packed the last of my notes in preparation for departure to Yap.

Several recurring patterns appear in this summary of events on Woleai in 1965 and it is reasonable to conclude this chapter with some generalizations that cover the more obvious areas of economic, political, and ceremonial activities.

In the sphere of subsistence, there is a distinct shift in exploitation that occurs during the breadfruit season. Furthermore patterns or emphases in marine exploitation vary from island to island according to the resource characteristics of the respective reef and lagoon areas that lie nearby. For example, setting surround nets for bonito is almost a weekly event on Falalus, but rarely occurs on Wottagai, only 3 miles away across the lagoon. Certainly one of the most striking features of economic pursuits, at least to the Western reader, is the distinct sexual separation in labor activities that occasionally involves direct competition of the sexes in some communal activity. When this occurs the competition is concluded by a form of gift presentation or exchange—cooked food from the women and drinking coconuts, sweet *falubwa* or fish from the men.

The above generalization can be extended further. Competition and cooperation between kin groups, districts, islands and "lagoons" are also characterized by similar ritual forms. These wider ceremonial occasions not only permit more equal distribution of surplus goods that may not be available at another location within the atoll (as during a *chúlifeimag* distribution of fish), but they may also serve (as during a symbolic funeral "exchange" of coconuts) to emphasize a certain island-wide or atoll-wide unit. Rituals and ceremonies on Woleai are invariably collective affairs meant to highlight solidarity and unity in an otherwise fragmented system of discrete social and political parts, and this is accomplished through the redistribution of resources.

Even at the wider levels of exchange, as during the installation of a new chief *(shufelu)* or within the context of the *sawei,* social collectives are emphasized. Gifts are offered to collectives, such as "Greater Lamotrek," a social group that may, in reality, not even have a representative on the island at the time of the ceremony. None the less, it is a unit that conceptually plays an important part in the overall order. The diary shows that at some level, with almost daily frequency, there occurs some ritual or ceremonial event that is meant to emphasize and symbolize this collective unity.

Proper order and ranked order are important to the people of Woleai: men/women, chiefs/commoners, taboo men/ordinary men, old men/young men. Each of these groups has its proper place and its proper behavior. Individual as well as collective decisions must take such status into account if someone, or more likely, some group, is not to be offended. On those occasions when a chief is placed in the position of disciplining an offender (quite likely someone who himself has ignored this proper order) he does so by imposing some collective prohibition. All men may be prohibited from drinking palm wine, or one island or kin group must pay a fine to another for the infractions of a single individual, or all youths are prohibited from returning to school because of the indiscretions of one. In this respect, at least, Woleai is at the opposite end of any spectrum that would include Western ideas concerning "cults of the individual," individual responsibility, and freedom. But certainly Woleai is none the poorer because of it.

This brings us to a final theme derived from the diary that should be mentioned. This is the conflict, perhaps incipient, that begins to appear between these Woleai patterns just summarized and the Western-American models associated with the Trust Territory administration. Several of the meetings discussed in the diary that were arranged according to traditional forms by chiefs exercising traditional powers were concerned with the new problems of schools, legislatures, and other governmental agencies. Requests were made of the people of Woleai by administrators to participate in these agencies, and the Woleai communities met to formulate a response via the traditional power structure and via traditional channels. They were not always successful in communicating their true feelings. Here is the genesis of intercultural conflict arising from inadequate communication between two contrasting ideological systems, neither of which fully understands the other. This is not the place to elaborate on the implications and ramifications of this situation, but the diary does show that the older Woleai leaders attempted on several occasions to "generalize" and interpret those problems that derive from interaction with foreign administrators (whether Yapese or American) in ways that corresponded to understood traditional patterns. Younger members of the community, in contrast, who had returned to Woleai after training in American-oriented boarding schools, tended to view the same situation from an "American" perspective. Here is the genesis of what is a more serious local cultural conflict that probably derives from the need to adapt to two differently conceived social environments—the more restricted traditional world of the older generation and the wider American-inspired "worldly" perspective of the younger generation. It is arguable which of these environments is the more important for the ultimate survival of the people of Woleai.

In any case, this summary of day-to-day events is generally representative of the subsistence-oriented adaptation common to the central and western Caroline islands of Micronesia. The cycles of activity on Eauripik, Ifaluk, and Lamotrek are quite similar. One reason for this, of course, is that the residents of all these islands share a common cultural heritage. Another reason is that all have adapted to a similar microenvironment, a setting within which a similar combination of variables operates. In other areas of the Pacific the choices particular communities have made to meet various challenges of coral island living have not been identical, but there are some similarities in the patterns that can be associated with identifiable coral island microenvironments.

Isolation is an important variable, not yet discussed in detail, that often serves to distinguish among specific kinds of microenvironments. The land mass and contiguous reefs of a particular atoll or raised coral island may not define the total ecosystem exploited by the atoll's inhabitants. Neighboring islands and reefs that lie within a reasonable distance also may be utilized and hence be a fundamental part of the supporting ecosystem. In some cases distance is the sole defining factor, but in others, distance combined with contrary winds, adverse currents, or lack of navigational expertise may effectively circumscribe the total exploitable region. The degree of isolation of a coral island very directly defines the total ecosystem. A range of possible systems thus can be conceived of as lying along a continuum. The end points of this continuum, perhaps more hypothetical than real, are represented by those coral islands totally isolated and consequently possessing precisely defined environmental boundaries at one extreme, and those islands at the other extreme that are in such proximity to a multitude of other coral or volcanic islands (or even continental land masses) that it is impossible to accurately define the limits of any system to which the inhabitants have adapted. For comparative purposes four points have been chosen on this continuum as representative of contrasting coral island microenvironments: *isolates, clusters, complexes,* and *fringing reef* islands. The adaptive necessities and possibilities of the four are significantly different and the cultural patterns associated with each reflect this.

Fringing reef islands are representative of the "fully integrated" end of the continuum. They lie within such proximity to volcanic islands that they are often referred to as "off-shore islands." There usually exists free and nearly unrestricted passage between the coral island and the volcanic "mainland," and thus the cultural patterns of the two groups are nearly identical. Coral island residents in this context usually speak the same language, fall within the same political organization, and share of the same resources as the residents of the nearby volcanic islands. Geographically these islands may either be parts of true fringing reef structures or geologically separate off-shore atolls or raised coral islands. Examples from Micronesia include Kayangel atoll, Peleliu, and Angaur, which lie off Babeldaob, Palau; Pis on the barrier reef of Truk; and possibly Ngulu south of Yap. In Polynesia similar examples are found in the Society Islands and among the smaller coral islands of Tonga (although in the latter case the main land masses are themselves extremely large raised coral islands). Other similar examples are found in Melanesia. In all of these the pattern of adaptation includes the larger land mass. Systems such as this, consequently, are somewhat peripheral to the main concern of this book, which is the examination of patterns of adaptation found in predominantly coral island settings.

At the opposite extreme from the fringing reef islands are those atolls and raised coral islands so isolated from other islands and archipelagoes that their residents are restricted to the limited ecosystem of the single island or atoll, its surrounding reefs, and ocean. In these cases isolation was determined by factors, individually or collectively, of location, contrary currents, unreliable winds, or limited navigational knowledge of the island's residents. In Micronesia the raised coral island of Nauru and the Polynesian outlier Kapingamarangi until recent times could be classified as this type of island. In Polynesia proper, Niue, Tongareva and to some extent Pukapuka were also solely dependent on their own resources. At various times in their histories other islands of Micronesia and Polynesia—Ujelang, Enewetak, Banaba, Arorae, Nukumanu, and possibly the abandoned Malden—might have qualified as isolates.

In other areas one finds a small number of coral islands and atolls lying in proximity to one another where the adaptation of the residents is not to a single island alone, but to the larger ecosystem of the coral island cluster. The various islands of a cluster are similar in productivity and potential. Consequently the differences between this ecosystem and that of the isolates is more one of quantity than quality. Such quantitative differences, however, may be crucial in times of environmental stress or disaster. Given the physiographic conditions that result in the formation of coral islands, clusters of islands, in fact, are more commonly found than are isolated islands.

In Micronesia, Abemama, Kuria, and Aranuka are one such cluster; Makin and Butaritari are another. In Polynesia, Manihiki and Rakahanga in the Northern Cook Islands and Nukunono, Atafu, and Fakaofu in the Tokelaus are all examples. In addition there once were several identifiable clusters in the Tuamotus which culturally were later assimilated into a larger sociopolitical system as Tahiti extended its control and influence into the area. Two such examples were Raroia-Takumé and Pukarua-Reao.

Finally, there are several areas of the Pacific where coral islands are part of a complex and extensive chain, occasionally either interspersed with volcanic islands or in proximity to high islands. In this situation there not only is diversity in island types and sizes—large and small atolls, raised coral islands, and perhaps the volcanic islands mentioned—but also often variation associated with microclimatic differences between islands in an extensive chain. Communities often took advantage of this diversity wherein adaptation was to an ecosystem that included qualitatively different parts. And cultural systems emerged that emphasized an interdependence between the dissimilar parts. Three examples of such complexes are first, the western and central Caroline coral islands and neighboring volcanic island of Yap; secondly, the Marshall Islands, all of which are coral islands but diverse since the archipelago is spread over a wide area; and lastly, in late aboriginal times, the northwestern Tuamotus and Tahiti.

In the next three chapters each of these types will be discussed in turn. The discussion will demonstrate, hopefully, that as the basic environmental system grows larger the cultural alternatives also multiply. Nevertheless, as the population increases to the limits of the carrying capacity of the system, however defined, the society often is faced with decreasing options so that, at certain critical points, the ultimate cultural choice within the complex may vary little in its basics from that of the isolate.

Fringes of a taro field. The woman, who is nearly hidden by the foliage, is harvesting Cyrtosperma. At the fringes of a taro field coconuts and other trees are often found interspersed with Colocasia and Cyrtosperma.

A man on Lamotrek returns with a morning's collection of palm-wine (*hachi*) tapped from two of his coconut trees.

Kite fishing. A man of Falalus, Woleai tests his breadfruit leaf kite before setting out to fish. A long line (held in his left hand) is attached to the tail of the kite and at the end of this line is a hook which skims along the surface of the water thereby attracting fish.

Woleai intra-atoll exchange gift. A man from Iur district Falalap arrives at
Falalus with a chulifeimag gift of fish.

Tallying coconuts for a funeral exchange. Several men on Falalus proceed through the district gathering coconuts into "groups of ten" (iaf) for a funeral exchange with Wottagai.

Sailing to a shufelu. The men of the western lagoon on Woleai sail to Falalap to participate in the installation ceremonies for a new chief on that island.

An Interisland sailing canoe. This canoe is underway within the lagoon of Lamotrek atoll. Note the ball-and-socket stepping of the mast.

Checking the measurements of a canoe hull. The men at each end hold a measuring line on designated control points and the third man marks areas in need of trimming.

A man trims the hull with an adze.

Bow view of a canoe hull under construction. Men on both sides trim the hull at points designated by the master canoe builder.

Attaching outrigger booms. An A-frame is set up to assist in attaching the outrigger booms. The measuring line held by the man is used to insure the booms are square to the hull.

Opposite page:
Adzing a canoe end-piece. This master canoe builder is using an adze with a special handle for deep work on such end pieces and within the keel section.

Framework of a roof for a dwelling. The skeleton of a roof including main plates, tie beams, king posts, ridgepole, and rafers are all tied together on the ground.

The same framework with thatch rafters and purlins added.

The framework is lifted into place on top of the houseposts.

The roof is thatched with plaited coconut fronds.

Divining by knots (*bwe*). Early in the morning, three men gather to divine an important event.

Divination knots. A diviner engaged in tying knots into coconut frond pinnae strips.

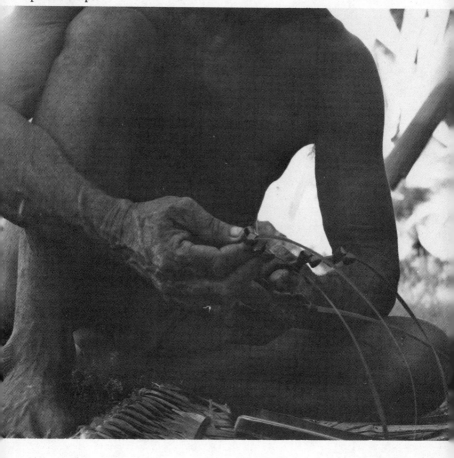

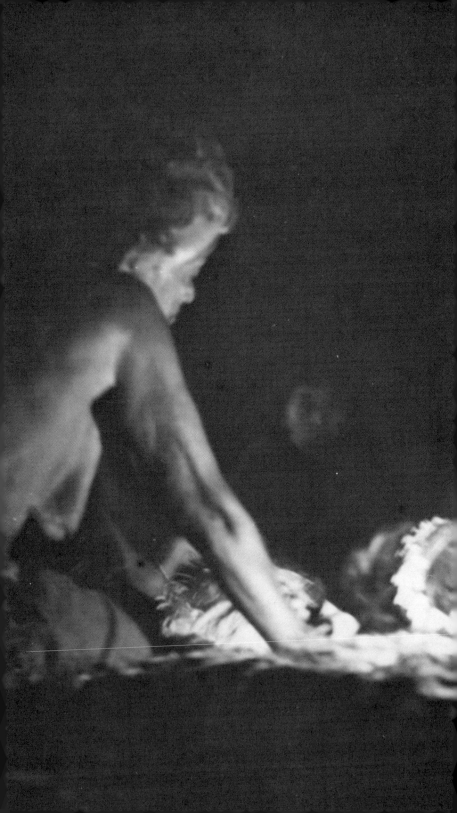

Opposite page:
Death and mourning. Most residents of the island gather in the canoe house where the body lies and participate in wailing and singing of dirges throughout the night until burial the next morning.

Receiving ceremonial shares. This man is receiving his share of a food distribution at a funeral feast.

Returning home with shares. After a funeral feast these women carry
home their household's share of the food gifts.

Chapter 4

CORAL ISOLATES

In pre-European times most of the evidence suggests that epidemics did not play a significant role in controlling population growth on the Pacific islands of Micronesia and Polynesia (Pirie 1972: 190). Because of this, and referring again to the examples cited in chapter 2, it seems reasonable to assume that even in aboriginal times the rate of population growth was between 1 and 3 percent per year in the absence of cultural controls. In some cases the natural controls of disease and accident may have been sufficient to keep population size within the carrying capacity of the isolated island; in most they probably were not.

In those cases where these controls were insufficient a short-term solution to food shortages that followed lay in the area of intensification of production and diversification of crops and resource exploitation. This might involve incorporation of normally unexploited areas into the horticultural or fishing spheres. The choice of this option probably meant short-term relief, since continued population growth ultimately would overtax the circumscribed resource area of the isolated island. And, if factors of environmental stress resulted in unexpected fluctuations in productivity, the situation could rapidly become acute. Social and cultural choices would have to be made to effect a solution. Examples of such choices can best be seen by discussing specific isolated coral islands.

KAPINGAMARANGI

This atoll (1° 5' N., 154° 41' E.) lies nearly 200 miles south of Nukuoro, its nearest neighbor, and more than 300 miles south of the Caroline archipelago. The atoll has a land area of 0.52 square miles, divided between 33 islets (Map 4). Most of its residents live on Werua and Souhou islands, although the other islands are exploited for coconuts and pandanus. The lagoon is 22 square miles in area. Kapingamarangi lies south of any reliable tradewinds and although its average annual rainfall is estimated to be 80 inches, the equatorial locale means the island is subject to periodic droughts. Furthermore the unreliable winds may have contributed to isolating the island by restricting the possibilities of reaching and leaving the area by sailing canoes. According to Michael Lieber (1968: 16) there is no evidence of interisland travel by Kapingamarangi people until the 1880s and the advent of the Spanish administration of Micronesia. Other evidence also indirectly supports this conclusion, specifically the events that followed the arrival of two different canoe loads of castaways that did arrive on the island.

The first canoe, which apparently arrived at the atoll about 150 years ago, was from Woleai. The Kapingamarangi residents were awed by the Woleaians' magical abilities and, based on Hambruch's information gathered in 1910, were in fact first introduced to a comprehensive set of navigational techniques by these castaways (Emory 1965: 51, 341). In the early 1870s a second canoe arrived at the island, this time from the Marshalls. These voyagers, apparently less grateful to their hosts than were the Woleaians, set about slaughtering three-fourths of the Kapingamarangi population before departing the island. In both cases one could conclude that, had the Kapingamarangi people themselves been accustomed to interisland travel or visitors, they probably would not have been so impressed and influenced by the Woleaians or deceived and unprepared for the Marshallese.

In 1910 the population of the atoll was 311 individuals. When Emory visited the island in the late 1940s and early 1950s it was about 500, which translates into a population density of between 1200 and 1300 individuals per square mile. Emory estimated the comfortable carrying capacity of the atoll at around

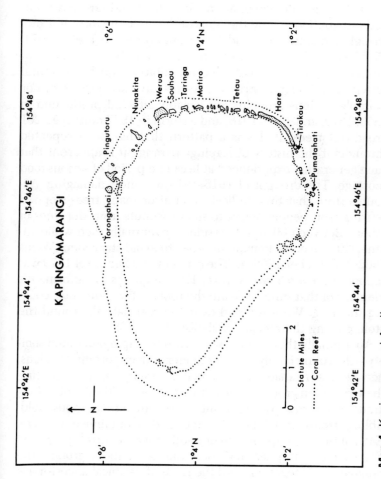

Map 4 Kapingamarangi Atoll

71

450 residents. "Above that figure, the strain on the economy becomes increasingly felt" (1965: 66).

Traditionally, subsistence on Kapingamarangi depended on pandanus (fresh and preserved), coconuts, breadfruit, taro, and diversified marine exploitation. Breadfruit and taro have limited distribution among the islets of the atoll, the former grows on eighteen of the islets and the latter only on five (Lieber 1974: 75). The availability of ground water and the occurence of drought impose the most severe limitations on horticultural activities, although destructive storms have also occurred. For example, serious droughts appreciably affected production in 1850, 1879, and 1916–1918, and a storm in 1947 destroyed 201 breadfruit trees. If this is a pattern that has been repeated throughout the history of Kapingamarangi, it is apparent that each generation experienced at least one period of serious food shortage. The drought of 1916–1918 was most damaging. Accounts from that time indicate that after many trees stopped bearing fruit people began to steal coconuts from the trees of others. Between 60 and 90 residents eventually died while another 90 moved to Ponape in order to avoid starvation (Wiens 1962: 158; Lieber 1968: 4). The drought and famine of 1879 was supposedly even more severe. Emory quotes an informant's memory of that time: "We ate the roots of the Pandanus, cooking them. . . . We wandered over the reef flats all around the atoll, picking them clean of shells" (1965: 132).

Aboriginally there were two classes in Kapingamarangi society—the ruling family and commoners. All important decisions, however, were made by a council of senior men representing the various kin groups of the island. Lieber (1968: 85) noted four kinds of kin groups important on the island: the household, sibling group, matrilineal lineage, and nonunilinear ramage. Each of these groups, in one or another way, controls property. For example, the last and most diffuse of these groups, the ramage, holds together until the lands of its apical ancestor are divided among descendants. Then segmentation of the ramage usually occurs. Emory (1965: 119, 130) emphasizes that nearly all land is held privately and that ownership and use rights of these various kin groups are "constantly being disputed" as well as the property boundaries themselves. He believes the incidence of these disputes increased as population pressures increased. Lieber (1974: 72), on the other hand, disagrees, "although land disputes are common their incidence does not correlate in any way with population growth." Perhaps these two authorities appear to disagree because they are talking about two different times and situations. Emory is referring to a time when the population of the atoll was near 500 and Lieber to a time when it was near 400. Furthermore Lieber is referring to a time when the option of moving to Ponape was both more practical and feasible than at the time of Emory's study shortly after World War II. Consequently, Lieber's comment (1974: 72) that "In fact almost all of the cases of current land litigation originated two or three generations ago" may not directly address the questions raised by his first statement. Certainly Kapingamarangi had reached its population maximum at other times in the precontact past, before the option of emigration to Ponape existed, and before relief supplies from an administering authority could be relied upon. It is quite reasonable to expect, then, that nearly all land disputes have their origins in earlier times. The question that is not answered is whether during times of population pressure the *overt* expression of these otherwise *dormant* disputes becomes more frequent.

Lieber (1974: 81) did find that although land could be held by individuals or corporate groups, most residents "prefer" individual ownership. Disputes over land could result in family fights and a landholder could even deny others right-of-way over his land. Fights also occurred between various men's house groups over fishing rights to particular reef and lagoon areas. These latter disputes ceased after the significant reduction in population caused by the Marshallese slaughter of the 1870s. The number of men's houses, themselves, was reduced from nine in 1870 to two by 1920. Extremely scarce resources, especially timber for canoe construction, were either directly (drift logs) or indirectly (locally grown breadfruit trees) controlled by the chiefs. For example, breadfruit tree owners could not cut down their trees without the permission of the chief and the chief priest. Over a considerable period of time the Kapingamarangi community has also been gradually expanding the acreage devoted to taro cultivation.

There is general agreement that all individuals "have a multiplicity of options regarding rights to various plots of land"

(Lieber 1974: 89). And that here, as in most other areas of Oceania, individuals attempt to exercise those rights that will result in the greatest, most stable, or more needed return. In times of shortages the chances increase that overlapping claims and rights will lead to open disputes.

In times of overpopulation it is thus understandable that internal policing increased. In addition, three other cultural practices became common: (1) abortion; (2) lengthening of time between pregnancies; and (3) postponement of marriage until a later-than-normal age (Emory 1965: 174, 155–156). And finally Lieber reports that during the 1916–1918 drought and famine an additional control was accepted at the suggestion of a Japanese who lived on the island, that of dissolving extant marriages as a further means of limiting the number of births.

NAURU

Nauru is a raised coral island isolated by location, prevailing currents, and the minimal seafaring ability of its inhabitants. This island, like Kapingamarangi, has an equatorial locale, lying less than one degree south of the equator, but unlike Kapingamarangi it is inhabited by a Micronesian speaking population.

The area of the island is 7.7 square miles and its interior rises to an elevation of 200 feet above sea level. In traditional times only the coastal fringe, a strip some 300 to 400 feet wide, along with an area contiguous to Buada lagoon where horticulture was possible, were inhabited (Map 5). The present day population of the island is some 4000, but aboriginally it apparently ranged between 2000 and 3000, resulting in an overall population density of 300 to 400 individuals per square mile. However, if one deducts the unproductive interior of the island from the computation, the actual density of the life-supporting coastal coconut fringe, an area of some 2.5 square miles, would approach 1000 persons per square mile.

Rainfall may exceed 80 inches per year, but droughts are an ever-present threat, as they are in the neighboring central and southern Gilbert Islands. In the recorded past droughts of more than a year in length have occurred in 1917–1919, 1937–1939, and 1949–1951 (Catala 1957: 3). In all of these periods rainfall averaged less than 5 inches per year. These droughts were all

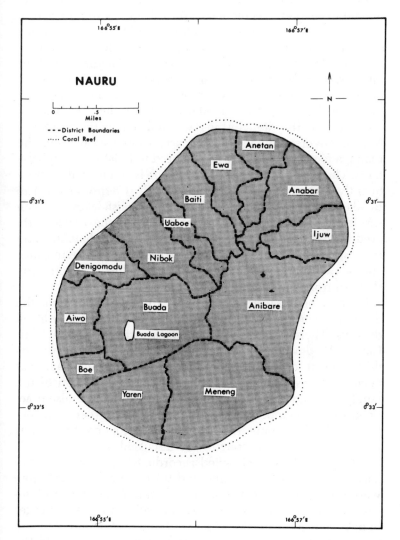

Map 5 Nauru Island

the more severe because of the raised nature of the island. Grimble's description of a prolonged drought on Banaba, quoted in chapter 1, could have applied equally well to Nauru.

In aboriginal times Nauruans primarily subsisted on coconuts and pandanus. The former were restricted to the coastal fringe, but the latter also grew in some parts of the higher and drier interior. Both dried coconut meat (copra) and pandanus were preserved and stored for later consumption. Coconut toddy, the sap gathered by tapping the inflorescence of the tree, was also important in the diet. Fishing was difficult in the waters of Nauru. Adverse currents could carry canoes away from the island, a fact that certainly contributed to isolating the inhabitants. The fringing reef surrounding the island is small. Consequently, Nauru residents raised milkfish (*Chanos chanos*) in Buada lagoon and a number of smaller brackish lakes found on the island. The procedure involved transferring larvae gathered from the fringing reef to holding ponds for hatching and the resulting fry to larger lakes where they were harvested after one or two years. Women also put great effort into gathering shellfish from the reef.

Nauruan houses were grouped in scattered hamlets along the coast and were included in one of fourteen different political districts. There were matrilineal clans within the society but Camilla Wedgwood (1936) believed their function was primarily limited to control of marriage. Cross-cousin marriage was encouraged as a means of insuring "greater cohesion of the family" (Wedgwood 1936: 382). Infant betrothal was also practiced among members of the upper class and agreements concerning land, coconut trees, and other property that a girl would bring into a marriage were discussed.

Real property was classified according to use—house sites, coconut land, pandanus land, and waste land. The last three were distinct ecological zones proceeding from shore to interior. Fish ponds were also owned and subdivided. Boundaries of both land and ponds were marked by stones, and these were often contested and the subject of protracted disputes. In the case of fish ponds caretakers were designated who watched over the boundary markers and the fish, guarding against encroachment and theft.

Wedgwood emphasized the individuation of ownership on

Nauru, "in no sense were ... homesteads clan property; they were individually owned and might even pass into the possession of a member of another clan—for in Nauru both men and women own land and give it ... to both sons and daughters and even unrelated friends" (1936: 374). Although any of these types of transfer were possible most homestead land passed from mothers to daughters with the eldest daughter exercising control and possessing the right to impose restrictive taboos over exploitation (Wedgwood 1936: 21). Property rights were often finely divided. On Nauru, as in several other areas of the Pacific, ownership rights were often separated so that the rights to parcels of land might be quite separate from the rights to the trees that grew upon the parcels. Rights in fish ponds could be similarly divided; a caretaker might have secondary rights compared to someone else, whose privileged position was symbolized by his right to eat the first fish taken from it.

Traditionally, Nauruan society was divided into three classes, the *temonibe* who were individuals descended from the eldest daughter of a clan foundress; the *amenengame* commoners who were descended from the younger daughters of the foundress; and lastly the *itsio,* a group of serfs who most commonly were individuals who had fled their home villages during warfare and had subsequently placed themselves under the protection of a higher-status landholder of some other hamlet or district.

Competition was a distinct theme in Nauruan society. Youths frequently participated in individual and group competitions in dancing, singing, boxing, wrestling, snipe or sandpiper fighting, kite flying, model canoe racing, story telling, string-figure manipulation, club throwing, chanting, ball hitting, tern and frigate bird trapping, and manufacture of *edongo* (preserved pandanus). In many of these activities groups toured the various districts of the island in order to participate in scheduled competitions. In other cases the competition was individually measured against set standards, as in the capture of frigate birds. A boy was expected to catch at least 40 of these birds before he could marry. Cooperation, on the other hand, was less common, especially outside of family groups. Cooperative fishing, for example, was limited to infrequent torch fishing expeditions for flying fish and seine net drives.

A competitive theme was also manifested in political maneuverings. Wedgwood believed that the various district heads were autonomous until the late 1800s or early 1900s, each head attempting to attract followers, perhaps from neighboring districts, as a means of increasing his prestige and power. The occasional castaway from the Gilbert Islands who arrived at Nauru, for example, might be taken under the protection of a district chief, although it was also the case that he might be killed.

Subsequent to European contact with the island, historical documents indicate that interhamlet and interdistrict competition, feuding, and warfare increased. The precise reasons for this are not clear, but a growing population and a resulting intensification of competition for land and resources seem to have been involved. Victories in warfare led to inequalities in land distribution, especially as far as the smaller and weaker clans were concerned. Political stratification and centralization of authority also intensified, leading to the emergence of two opposing alliances. The first included the districts of Ijuw, Anabar, Anetan, Ewa, Baiti, Uaboe, and Nibok; and the second Anibare, Meneng, Yaren, Boe, and Aiwo. Denigomodu and Buada, the two remaining districts, vacillated in their affiliation depending on the nature of the dispute at hand and the persuasiveness of relatives of one or the other alliance. Conflict reached its height on the island after alcohol and guns were introduced by Europeans and a ten-year war between the districts was not ended until German colonial intervention in 1888.

NIUE

In size, Niue is atypical of the usual coral island. It is some 100 square miles in area and thus considerably larger than any other island treated in this book (Map 6). Nevertheless as a coral island it possessed similar characteristics and was subject to many of the same limitations as most of the smaller raised coral islands. The average elevation of the island is similar to that of Nauru, some 220 feet above sea level. The island's nearest neighbor is Vavau in the Tonga chain, 240 miles to the west. Geographically and culturally Niue is an island of Polynesia.

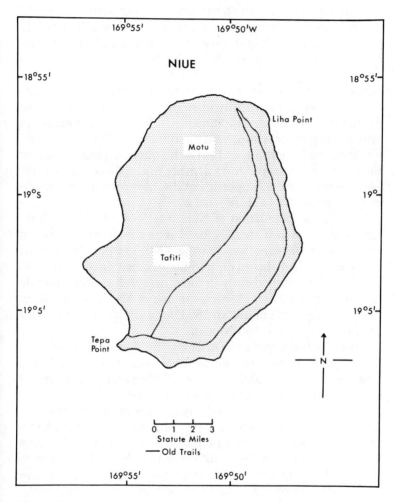

Map 6 Niue Island

The average annual rainfall here is a moderate 60 inches, but it is seasonally distributed so that most falls during the months of December and January. Consequently, "nearly every year a drought occurs, when the taro wilts and is devoured by insects" (Loeb 1926: 6). Edwin Loeb, in fact, goes on to say "most of the peculiar features of Niue culture, economic, social and religious, have developed as a result of the frequent occurrence of drought." The island lies on the edge of the southern Pacific hurricane belt and experiences tropical storms on the average of once every ten years. Breadfruit is a relatively recent introduction to the island. Traditionally, subsistence depended on taro, arrowroot, coconuts, yams, and bananas. The first of these was the most important, and as Loeb's quote suggests it was also the crop most susceptible to damage during droughts. On this island some of the most persistent disputes concerned rights to water (Crocombe 1971: 68).

In 1875 the population of Niue was 5080; thereafter it declined more or less steadily until it began to grow again in recent times, once more surpassing 5000. The population maximum of the island, based on traditional subsistence techniques, was probably reached early in the nineteenth century, and the decline that set in was a consequence of Western-introduced diseases and slave raiding. In 1863, for example, Peruvian slavers carried off some 150 Niueans.

Given a total population of 5000, the density is a comparatively low 50 persons per square mile. As in the case of Nauru, however, the exploitable land area of Niue realistically is much smaller than its total area, the most productive land forming a narrow coastal fringe. Since the early part of this century most Niueans have lived within a mile of the coast. In earlier times, during the years of Niue's population maximum and isolation from any reliable contact with other islands, settlements were dispersed throughout the island in bush areas and even caves as a defensive response to fears of attack from neighboring settlements. Of all the islands thus far discussed, Niue seems to have suffered most from chronic warfare and feuding.

The marginal nature of production overtaxed the carrying capacity of the island's poor soil. The shortages that inevitably followed must have intensified competition for productive land and subsequently led to open conflict. An early observer noted that residents were having to extend cultivation into areas quite distant from villages and he surmised that "it is through this process of clearing that a good deal of the island is now in scrub, or a second growth of wood" (as quoted by Loeb 1926: 7). In addition the periodic droughts resulted in competition for taro land and access to reliable water sources, and increased disputes over control of fruit bearing trees.

Fishing was difficult and poor off the island, an observation supported in part by the fact that here, as on Fais, fishermen actively hunted sharks. Niue possesses a very limited reef area and apparently the islanders' navigational skills were not elaborate. Loeb (1926: 99) refers to two stories of fishing fleets that were blown away from the island by contrary winds and in only one of the accounts is mention made of sails on the canoes. The common craft of the islanders apparently were six- or four-seated paddling canoes. Although a Niuean folktale refers to a land bridge that once connected the island to Tonga, the latter was a place name that was applied to any foreign place. In reality the isolation of the island meant that, as with the other islands considered in this section, problems of resource shortages, population pressures, and environmental stress had to be handled internally.

Marriages were often arranged on Niue in order to gain access to land or to strengthen alliances between neighboring settlements. A couple took up residence where their chances of economic gain were greatest. Land was held by what Loeb terms "the family," which seems to have been an ambilineal group sharing a common residence. A degree of patri-emphasis was apparent in that authority within the group was generally based on male primogeniture. In those times when warfare was common and residences were dispersed, exchange relations developed that served to tie together the scattered households of a "family." Those individuals who lived near the sea devoted most of their time to fishing and exchanged their surplus fish for taro produced by their inland relatives. Genealogies were relatively shallow on Niue, compared to many other Polynesian communities, and this contributed to a general flexibility in determining legitimate claims to land and leadership.

Niueans recognized three classes, the *toa* warriors; *fekafekau* commoners or servants of the warriors; and *lalo tagata*, low people. Apparently individual ability determined membership in the *toa* class. Strength and ability could raise a man to warrior rank and if he were able to attract a number of followers (*fekafekau*) he could become a leader or chief within this class. During the course of the eighteenth and nineteenth centuries power began to crystallize around two centers at opposite ends of the island. These two endogamous divisions, Motu and Tafiti, became the focus for much of the warfare, the general purpose of which was to obtain land from the opposing alliance.

At a somewhat later date a single symbolic authority emerged in the form of a paramount chief (Loeb believes the idea was imported from Tonga). Nevertheless, warfare between alliances continued to occur under the leadership of district chiefs and this, in combination with the fact that the paramount chief or "king" (*patuiki*) could be selected from among generally unimportant men, suggests that the office was primarily symbolic. Apparently the most important event in the reign of a king was his death. The *patuiki* was held responsible for the welfare of the Niueans; he was believed to have power over the weather and the growth of crops. Therefore in times of drought and famine the king was ceremoniously killed "for neglect of duty" (Loeb 1926: 55).

In addition to warfare and famine several other mechanisms of population control operated. These included specified periods of time when sexual intercourse was taboo, abortion, and a form of gerontocide, wherein the aged and infirm might be abandoned to die in the bush. Infanticide generally was not practiced except in times of war when a persistently crying child might be killed in order that the hiding place of a family not be revealed to a raiding party of enemies. Finally, a unique feature of Niuean society that also served to reduce population numbers was a form of institutionalized suicide related to warfare. In this case it was common for many individuals on the losing side of a battle to subsequently commit suicide. If we add these deaths to those that actually occurred in battle and finally add yet another group of suicides who took their lives as an expression of grief at the death of a relative (another institutionalized practice) one can conclude that warfare and the cycle of deaths that followed a battle must have played a significant role in population control.

TONGAREVA

This atoll of Polynesia is composed of fifteen separate islets, eight of which are large enough to support permanent residents (Map 7). Its total land area is about 6 square miles. From the time this atoll was sighted in the nineteenth century by Otto von Kotzebue, population estimates have varied. Kotzebue counted 36 canoes that came out to meet him, each carrying between 7 and 13 people. Assuming an equal number of residents were left ashore the population at that time could have been anything from 600 to 1200. Peter Buck (1932a: 9) estimated the pre-European population at about 2000, which equals a density of 300 to 400 individuals per square mile. In recent years the atoll has supported about 610 permanent residents. In traditional times the inhabitants of Tongareva apparently were skilled seamen and navigators. According to John Wilkes, who visited the island in the early 1800s these islanders constructed the largest canoes of any low island society he visited. Tongareva's location, however, prevented frequent or sustained contact with neighbors, the nearest of which is Rakahanga, more than 200 miles to the southwest.

The average annual rainfall is a moderate 71 inches, with frequent deviation from this mean. Rainfall in the wettest year recorded totalled more than 150 inches, while in the driest only 36 inches fell (Wiens 1962: 155). Tongareva is not a rich atoll and this is undoubtedly related to the erratic rainfall pattern. The island however is not usually subject to destructive tropical storms.

The main subsistence crops are coconuts and pandanus. Colocasia, sweet potatoes, and even Cyrtosperma were not traditionally cultivated. The fisheries, as characteristic of an atoll this size, were quite rich. Numerous reef fish, shellfish, porpoises, and turtles were present although in Tongarevan society the latter two could only be consummed by men. Buck noted that he found nearly all the land of the atoll exploited in one or another way.

The basis of Tongarevan social organization was a bilateral kindred of the Polynesian ramage type. This kind of system possessed a degree of flexibility that would be advantageous for survival. A newly married couple could choose which kin group

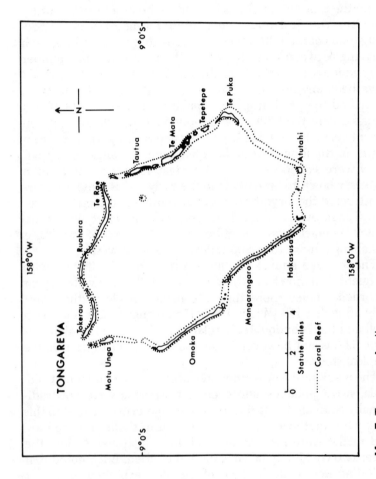

Map 7 Tongareva Atoll

to settle with, that of the wife or that of the husband, depending on potential economic advantage. This was a situation quite similar to that found on Niue. Such freedom of choice served to distribute a population more evenly over the atoll. After residential choice was made a couple and subsequently their children were absorbed into the local ramage with equal access to its lands (*kainga*). Buck further noted that the population was slowly expanding into new areas as these were converted to coconut production (1932a: 57). Traditionally, land tenure was closely identified with coconut cultivation. For example Buck states that the residents of one district "immediately pulled up any nuts planted near the boundaries by inhabitants of another division. To allow the trees to remain would have been to recognize rights of the owners of the trees to the land" (1932a: 58).

Tongareva was missionized in 1854 and conversion resulted in fundamental cultural changes. Previous to this date many traditional practices served to control consumption and distribution of scarce resources. Three of the more important were feuding, raiding, and the *masanga*.

The *masanga* was a taboo that could be imposed forbidding exploitation of designated coconut trees. It was usually invoked in order to allow overexploited trees a period of recovery. A *masanga* could be declared by an individual over his own trees or, more importantly, by a community over all of its holdings. During a period of population maximum a *masanga* imposed by one community could precipitate feuding and warfare with another. Lamont (1867: 273) details one such example. In the mid-1860s a *masanga* was declared by the residents of Mangarongaro on the south side of the atoll. Owing to an epidemic on that island, most of the coconuts of the district had been consumed in the course of mortuary feasts. The *masanga* was invoked so that the remaining nuts could mature and the trees replenish themselves. The residents of this district, in order to avoid starvation, soon after began a campaign of raiding the coconut plantations of neighboring islands. These raids naturally precipitated warfare between the islands.

All islands and districts were continually vigilant against such raids. Interdistrict visiting within the atoll was controlled by strict protocol and caution, and was subject to continual observation. If one crossed a boundary between two districts without acknowledging the formalities, the infringement could result in open hostilities since it was assumed the crossing was the initial step of a raid. The old women and young children of the settlements maintained a watch over the coconut trees of their district. Consequently, it was virtually impossible for anyone to climb a tree undetected. And if a man did climb a tree that belonged to someone else, the cries of the guards quickly brought armed men to the spot. If a raiding party were caught in this manner the hostilities might begin with an exchange of stones and spears followed by hand-to-hand fighting. A skirmish of this type could then provoke district level hostilities or even confrontations between larger alliances of districts.

PUKAPUKA

Pukapuka is probably one of the most productive of Polynesian coral isolates. It lies in the northern Cook group and has nearly 2 square miles of land area divided between three islands (Map 8). The nearest neighboring inhabited islands are Rakahanga and Manihiki, 200 miles to the east, and Samoa, some 390 miles southeast. The small uninhabited coral island of Nassau, 42 miles southeast of Pukapuka, was periodically exploited by the Pukapukans.

Pukapuka's high productivity is related to its high rainfall, more than 100 inches per year. The seasonal distribution is less distinct than is the case on Tongareva. The period from May to September is drier than that from October to April, but killing droughts are less common. Severe tropical storms are similarly uncommon although Wiens reports that in one year (1931) Pukapuka experienced 23 gales compared to an earlier record of 4 gales distributed over a period of 12 years. Tradition refers to a tidal wave that swept the island some 300 years ago. The vividness of this event in folklore suggests a catastrophe of some magnitude. Before this apparent tsunami the population of the atoll was estimated at between 1000 and 2000 individuals, which meant a density of 500 to 1000 persons per square mile. After the event the population was "reduced to 15 men and their families" (Beaglehole and Beaglehole 1938: 21). In January 1914 another tsunami swept the island and shortly thereafter 52 residents were moved to Rarotonga "in order to relieve

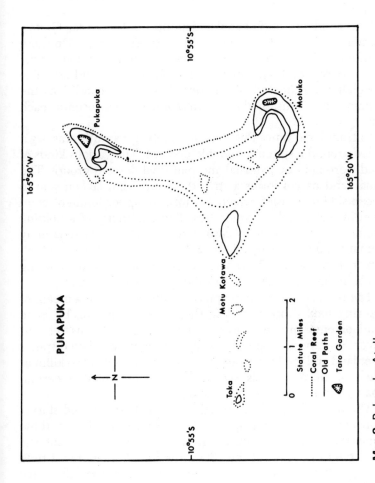

Map 8 Pukapuka Atoll

distress caused by the tidal wave" according to Ernest and Pearl Beaglehole. In 1935 the population of the atoll was 632 and in 1974, according to Julia Hecht, an ethnographer who was working on the island, there were a total of 760 individuals in residence.

The residents of Pukapuka depend on Colocasia, Cyrtosperma, and coconuts as their main subsistence crops. On those occasions when taro was scarce, that is, after a drought, tidal wave, or storm, the populace relied on coconuts and fish. The Beagleholes estimated that under these latter conditions the average adult consumed between seven and ten coconuts each day.

In traditional times Pukapukan society apparently was organized around a system of double descent. The various kinds of land were held by paternal and maternal descent groups. The usual land parcel forms a strip that runs from lagoon side to ocean side of an islet, which is a form of apportionment common in many atoll communities. The continuity of a holding might be interrupted by taro gardens, which are separately demarcated and allocated, or by the presence of so-called village reserve lands. These areas were set off from surrounding lands by lines of stones or in some cases walls of coral.

The reserve land system apparently developed as a means of assuring food supplies during shortages brought on by some kind of environmental stress. Pukapukan traditions recount several instances of famine and starvation, times when disputes over land and food culminated in intervillage feuds and killings. Each of these periods seems to have precipitated certain changes in the land tenure system.

The most outstanding periods of food shortages and starvation mentioned in Pukapukan folk history are tied to those times that followed a tsunami. In the first recounted event, the severe seismic wave of the 1600s, the island chief of that time decreed that all surviving residents should temporarily leave their villages and settle in Loto village where, presumably, their collective efforts might better guarantee survival. It is possible that the coconut reserve lands were established at about this time. Subsequent to this, and especially after the destructive wave of 1914, the island council confiscated several taro fields that were owned by individual lineages and divided them among all the people of the island in order to carry the community over the food shortage caused by the wave (Beaglehole and Beaglehole 1938: 32). This latter action apparently later led to the designation of some of these plots as community taro fields. At the time of the Beagleholes' research these taro gardens were subdivided into areas for men, women, and children, and the plots were annually redistributed to coincide with the demographic changes in the resident population.

Both the taro and coconut reserves were patrolled by guards (*pule*). Their day-to-day responsibilities were to man guard houses and check points, and to patrol reserve lands in an attempt to keep thievery to a minimum. "Though all believe that stealing from the reserve is immoral, few Pukapukans are above helping themselves to nuts in secret" (Beaglehole and Beaglehole 1938: 37). Such thievery was common even though it was believed that in addition to secular fines theft might also result in sickness, which was an ultimate punishment sent by the gods of the island. In addition once each month the guards closely inspected reserve areas and had the authority to fine community members who failed to keep their allotments free of weeds. The village council could decide when to relax or increase restrictions on reserve lands. During periods of extreme food shortage, as after a tsunami, the council could decree *pule pae,* thereby giving reserve guards the authority to execute by drowning or strangulation anyone caught stealing from the reserve lands.

Fishing grounds and reefs were divided among the three villages of the atoll. Trespassers who were caught fishing in another village's area were fined by the apprehending guards. Occasionally a village would declare its lagoon or reef reserves open to the other two villages. The residents who took advantage of this opening presented gifts of taro and coconuts to the host villagers.

Pukapuka atoll was somewhat less isolated than the other islands discussed in this chapter. Pukapukan traditions tell of travel to Niue, Upolu, Samoa, and the Gilbert and Ellice islands, but such travel, by any measure, was dangerous and infrequent. More regular contact, however, was maintained with the uninhabited island of Nassau. In post-European contact times only travel to Nassau was still undertaken and consequently it was only this island that had any continuing direct effect on the adaptation of the Pukapukans. The Pukapukans have long claimed "ownership" of Nassau and in 1951 formalized this with the administering authority when they purchased the island from the New Zealand government. In earlier times the island was used as a fishery and turtling area while in post-contact times, during periods of overpopulation or food shortages, colonists from Pukapuka have temporarily moved to Nassau. For some time, then, this small island has been a part of the supporting ecosystem of the Pukapukans. Canoe transportation was essential for this purpose. Consequently, each patrilineage attempted to have at least one seaworthy craft at hand at all times. Special taboos could be placed on trees in order to reserve them as timber for canoe construction.

SUMMARY

Overpopulation and the maintenance of some form of homeostasis were problems that commonly affected isolated coral islands. Population pressures led to intensified horticultural efforts, which in some cases overtaxed the carrying capacity of the land. Food supplies could also fluctuate significantly during periods of environmental stress.

All of the isolate societies attempted, at various times, to increase production through exploitation of more and more marginal lands. Wherever environmental conditions permitted, subsistence production was based on crop diversification. All islands relied heavily on coconuts and most exploited pandanus as well. Kapingamarangi, Pukapuka, and Nuie put special effort into taro cultivation. Kapingamarangi could rely, to some extent, on breadfruit, and Niue on arrowroot. Nevertheless factors of environmental stress, most frequently drought, periodically resulted in resource shortages on all of these islands. Typhoons or hurricanes and tsunami were less frequently cited as causes for food shortages.

Such shortages have frequently been followed by periods of increasing competition for available food and in several cases by starvation. This is reflected in a common developmental pattern wherein disputes over land ownership and boundaries were followed by expropriation or theft of produce. These actions often escalated to feuds and occasionally full-scale warfare. Several of these isolate societies instituted other cultural responses to resource shortages that delayed or eliminated open hostilities by recognizing a flexible or changing system of tenure.

The underlying pattern of land and resource control common in Oceania was based on corporate control. Kin groups, either lineages or ramages, held land jointly and reallocated it among the group's members for exploitation and use. The ramage form of organization, of course, often permits one to claim membership in more than one landholding group. Alliances of various types could also increase an individual's options. For example on both Nauru and Niue a stated consideration in negotiation of marriages was possible access to resource areas the marriage would permit. Periods of resource shortages brought both internal and external pressures on these groups for redistribution. Collectivization or further individuation of holdings were contrasting options. By *individuation* is meant the transfer of effective control from the larger corporate units into the hands of smaller sub-units, as at one point happened in the case of Kapingamarangi, or ultimately into the hands of individuals, as reported for Nauru. In Tongareva the *masanga,* when imposed individually, reflected a similar conceptualization of rights over land and resources. But the *masanga* could precipitate thievery and feuding. On Pukapuka objectives similar to those of the *masanga* were achieved in a different manner with a different emphasis. Here it was normal to have certain reserve areas continuously closed to exploitation, to be opened only in times of emergency. This was probably a more effective solution to the problems of resource shortages, in part because this collectivization tended to minimize conflict to a greater degree than did individuation of tenure. In both of these cases, as well as on Nauru, restrictions over exploitation were enforced by institutionalized guard systems.

In general Kapingamarangi society responded to population —resource pressures in a different way. Abortion, infanticide, delayed marriages, and post-partum sexual taboos were invoked and undoubtedly helped control population numbers. Niue similarly permitted abortion and in addition gerontocide, king killing, and institutionalized suicide, all of which were more frequent during periods of food shortage. Cultural controls, such as these, could result in a period of secondary population decline above and beyond any initial decline related to food scarcity and starvation.

Furthermore in the cases of Niue and Nauru social conflict was also common. Small scale feuding and raiding were found in both societies and increased to a level of open and prolonged warfare in times of serious resource shortages. Warfare encouraged development of protective alliances. Twelve of the fourteen districts on Nauru were grouped into two opposing alliances, roughly corresponding to the northern and southern halves of the island. The two remaining districts vacillated in their affiliation depending on the nature of the dispute and the persuasiveness of relatives within one or the other alliance. The warfare of Niue similarly led to the emergence of the two opposing centers of Motu and Tafiti.

Social ranking was manifest in all of these isolate societies, most commonly expressed as classes of chiefs and commoners. In none, however, was there full centralization of authority in a single office or political district, although the alliances on Niue and Nauru suggest developments in this direction. It might be noted that these were the two islands with the most severe periodic resource shortages.

Figure 5 attempts to schematically represent the variables and their relationships in the isolate ecosystem as described in this chapter. The three primary loops of this diagram represent sequences of events in maintaining a stable community in the face of increasing population and/or resource shortages. Loop 1 depends on the natural controls of disease and accidental death, which apparently were not significant in precontact Polynesia and Micronesia. The important decision function of loop 2 is starvation. It seems likely that a stable community could be maintained by way of loop 2 only in those cases of a minor imbalance of people and resources since few societies would let starvation take its toll for very long before attempting to alleviate the situation through social action.

Loop 3 outlines the main social variables included in the adaptive strategies of coral isolates. All of the isolates attempted to meet the problems of population–resource imbalance through one or more of these courses of action: alterations in

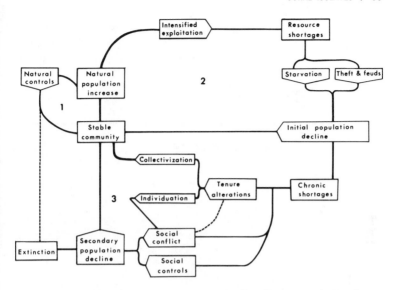

Figure 5 Simplified isolate system diagram. The diagram includes the main variables that tend to alter or maintain a stable community on a coral isolate (see text for detailed discussion).

tenure, social conflict (warfare), or social controls on rate of population growth (infanticide, abortion, and so on). These last two options inevitably led to a secondary population decline that might eventually restore a population–resource balance and a stable community. If the combined natural and social controls were not successful in restoring this balance, a fourth loop would lead to community extinction rather than community stabilization. However, since all of the cases described in this chapter were viable on-going communities, this loop represents a theoretical threat, knowledge of which may at various times in their histories have influenced the actions of residents of Kapingamarangi, Nauru, Niue, Tongareva, and Pukapuka.

Chapter 5

CORAL CLUSTERS

An adaptive strategy based on an ecosystem larger than a single island or small atoll potentially includes an increased number of cultural options. In most instances this expanded environmental system entails several atolls or raised coral islands, although in some cases a particularly large atoll with widely separated islets may provide a similar setting. Most commonly this kind of ecosystem is represented by a small cluster of islands of similar type and productivity lying within easy travelling distance of one another. The communities of the various atolls and islands normally function autonomously in day-to-day affairs, but in periods of population–resource imbalance their proximity to one another encourages economic exchange, personnel movements, or, on the negative side, interisland warfare and raiding. The clusters of Manihiki–Rakahanga, Nukunonu–Atafu–Fakaofo, Raroia–Takumé, Pukarua–Reao, and Makin–Butaritari represent a variety of cluster adaptations traditionally found in Polynesia and Micronesia.

MANIHIKI–RAKAHANGA

Peter Buck's 1932 study of these two atolls provides us with an outline of the traditional sociocultural system. The atolls are part of the northern Cook Islands and are separated from

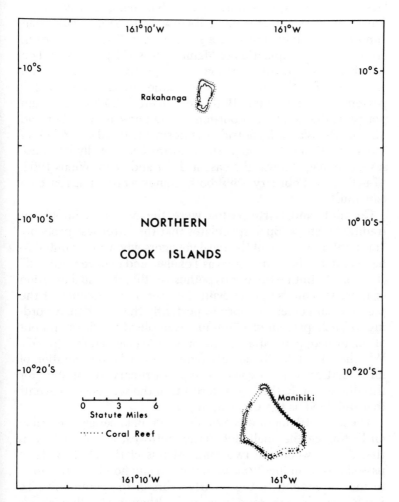

Map 9 Manihiki–Rakahanga, Northern Cook Islands

each other by 25 miles of open ocean (Map 9). Manihiki is the larger, possessing two large islets and a score of smaller ones, with a total land area of approximately 2 square miles and a lagoon some 11 square miles in area. Rakahanga has about 1½ square miles of land area divided between two major islets that almost completely surround a small lagoon 2 square miles in area. The 1906 population of Manihiki was 521 persons, and on Rakahanga 352. In 1971 the figures, respectively, were 556 and 329. These figures amount to a population density of some 250 persons per square mile. Both atolls average 95 inches of rain per year, the greater proportion falling between October and March. The islands lie outside the normal tropical storm belt of the south Pacific, although such storms occasionally do cause severe damage, as was the case in 1877 and 1905 (Wiens 1962: 474–475). In February 1899 both islands were damaged by a tsunami.

Coconuts and Cyrtosperma were the two most important traditional crops. Buck speculates that the latter was probably "brought in by some of the local voyagers who were reputed to have visited other lands, such as Tokelau, and to have returned" (193.ᵒᵇ: 84). But he further hypothesizes that the usual isolation of these two atolls may explain the precontact absence of the pig, dog, and chicken. More importantly this isolation, according to Buck, presented a "unique example of the development of an insular population from one biological family" (p. 57). Whether a single "biological family" or a larger number of initial settlers were involved is not of primary importance for this discussion. Rather our interest is in the sequence of events that unfolded as the population grew.

The first settlement was established on Rakahanga, ostensibly on Te Kainga, the small islet on the southwest side of the lagoon that lies between the two main islands of the atoll. As time passed new "families" *(puna)* emerged and houses were added to the settlement. In these early years of the community Te Kainga was the only residential area, although the other islands of the atoll were utilized for food production.

Descent was reckoned bilaterally, but from an early date the community organized itself dualistically according to descent from one or the other of two founding brothers, Matangaro and Hukutahu. Those members who claimed descent from

Matangaro established residence on the seaward side of Te
Kainga while those who emphasized descent from Hukutahu
built their houses on the lagoon side. Rights to chiefly title
(ariki) of the community were restricted to the Hukutahu line.
It seems likely, however, that the bilateral basis of descent reckoning permitted individuals to make choices in emphasizing
particular generational linkages in order to affiliate with the
moiety of their choice. Arranged marriages and adoptions were
common. Postmarital residence most commonly was virilocal.

The land of the atoll was divided between the moieties, and
particular sections of land were allocated to specific families for
use. The boundaries that set off one land parcel from another
"were, to a certain extent, created by the spreading and meeting of the coconut trees that had been planted by successive
generations" (Buck 1932b: 67). These family land boundaries
apparently were not permanently fixed and community decisions could reallocate holdings in each generation to take account of demographic shifts. The boundaries between moiety
holdings, however, were more permanently established and
were marked both within the village and in outlying areas.
According to Buck's calculations, after ten generations the
Hukutahu and Matangaro descent groups both underwent
fissioning so the community from that point on was structurally
divided into four units. And land was subsequently identified
with, and controlled by, one of these four *matakeinanga.* At the
time of Buck's study the original moiety division was still important in religious organization, each having its own shrine
(marae) within the village, while at another level, minor gods
were associated with each of the four descent groups. Each of
the latter also had its own set of food taboos.

At some point subsistence pressures obviously began to be
felt by the Rakahangans. Based on estimates of the present-day
carrying capacity of the atoll this most probably occurred when
the population reached a level of 600 to 700. At that time
various individuals began to plant the neighboring atoll of
Manihiki with coconuts and Cyrtosperma and an interesting
pattern of exploitation soon followed. "When food supplies ran
short on Rakahanga, the whole population voyaged across to
Manihiki to partake of the food which had been planted there"
(Buck 1932b: 65–66). Residence on Manihiki continued until

food supplies on that atoll grew short; then the population voyaged back to Rakahanga, the supplies of the latter atoll having replenished themselves in the interval.

Movements from one atoll to the other occurred on a regular basis although it is not entirely clear from Buck's account whether on every occasion the total population moved at one time or whether each of the four subdivisions travelled independently to Manihiki as each exhausted its resources on Rakahanga. Buck does note, however, that although weapons were present in the form of spears and clubs, there were no accounts in traditional narratives of warfare. He attributes this to the solidarity of the community fostered by the single community residential pattern.

The London Missionary Society introduced Christianity to the area in the early 1850s, and these missionaries successfully converted the population in less than a year. The missionaries also persuaded the Rakahangans to abandon their voyages following an accident in which 20 individuals were drowned during a storm on a trip from Manihiki. The missionaries' solution was to divide the population and permanently settle both islands.

TOKELAU ISLANDS

Nukunonu, Atafu, and Fakaofo are the three atolls of this Polynesian chain. Nukunonu is the largest and the centrally situated atoll of the group. Atafu is some 50 miles northwest and Fakaofo 35 miles southeast of Nukunonu (Map 10).

Nukunonu has an estimated land area of approximately 2 square miles divided between 3 large islets and some 40 smaller ones. The land area of Fakaofo is about 1 square mile divided between 50 islets. Atafu is the smallest with an area of 0.76 square miles, again divided between 40 or 50 islets. Their lagoon areas, respectively, are Nukunonu 30 square miles, Fakaofo 16 square miles, and Atafu about 5 square miles.

The earliest population estimates for two of the atolls date from the 1840s. Atafu was reported as having a population of 120 and Fakaofo some 600 people. The earliest population estimate for Nukunonu was made in 1863 and it reported that 140 individuals were resident on the atoll. The evidence suggests

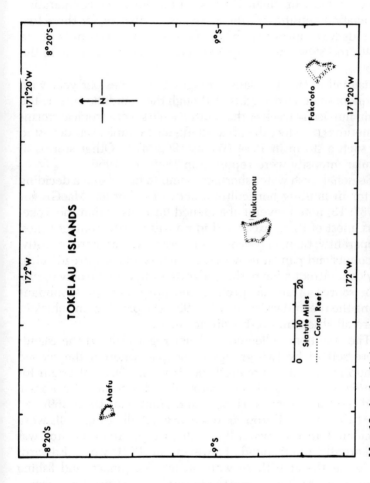

Map 10 Atafu, Nukunonu, and Fakaofo, Tokelau Islands

99

that there was a great amount of interatoll movement of residents even in those years. In modern times the resident populations reached peaks in the mid-1960s at which time Atafu supported 615 residents, Fakaofo 733, and Nukunonu 553 (Hooper and Huntsman 1973). Consequently, the comparative population densities for the Tokelaus, as a whole, for these two periods was approximately 230 persons per square mile in the 1840s to 1880s, and nearly 500 persons per square mile in the 1960s.

Rainfall in the Tokelaus averages 115 inches per year with frequent seasonal droughts. Although the islands lie outside the main hurricane track of the south Pacific severe tropical storms sometimes do affect the area. Atafu, for example, was devasted by such a storm in 1914 (Wiens 1962: 474). Other storms of similar intensity were reported in 1846 and 1966.

Seasonal fresh water shortages seem to have been a deciding factor in limiting horticultural activities. Gordon MacGregor (1937: 13) noted several abandoned taro pits within the Tokelaus, most of them excavated in post-European contact times. Apparently, then, in precontact times, as well as more recently, coconuts and pandanus were the dietary staples. Breadfruit is a recent introduction to these islands. Fish were the only significant source of animal protein and are reportedly abundant along the reefs (MacGregor 1937: 92). The pig, dog, and chicken were all absent in pre-European times.

The traditions collected by MacGregor claimed the islands were settled by two groups of people, wherein the second group of arrivals conquered the first. The place of origin for these migrants has been variously placed in Samoa, Rarotonga, and the Ellice Islands (Hooper and Huntsman 1973: 369).

At the time of European discovery not all of the atolls were inhabited. In 1765 when Byron discovered Atafu the atoll was apparently uninhabited. However, in 1791 when Edwards called at the atoll there were structures, canoes, and fishing gear present which suggested periodic and temporary occupation by fishing parties (MacGregor 1937: 30).

By 1820 groups of permanent colonists had arrived from Fakaofo. There is further evidence in traditional histories, however, that this was the second settlement of the atoll, the first inhibitants having been driven off or annihilated by war parties from Fakaofo previous to 1765. Apparently, following the settlement of all the Tokelaus, warfare was a continuing problem that affected settlement patterns. While discussing the population of Fakaofo, MacGregor noted that the residents were "forced in the past to live in one village for self-protection and to keep control of the food supply, the entire population has been able to confine itself to the small area only by extending the floor of the island over the lagoon" (1937: 5). There is some conflicting evidence regarding the extent of traditional interisland travel and navigational knowledge. On the one hand, as the above quotation suggests, there was an ever-present threat of attack from one of the neighboring atolls, but on the other hand, in 1841 Hale states that the residents of Atafu were unaware of any neighboring islands (as quoted by MacGregor 1937: 27). It seems likely, however, that Hale misunderstood his informants and that interatoll travel did occur with some frequency. It may even have been the case that irregular contact ranged as far as some of the more distant islands of Polynesia, but the effects of this were negligible. For all practical purposes the Tokelau residents were entirely dependent on the ecosystem circumscribed by the three atolls.

Each island was governed by a chief and a council composed of kindred heads. Status within the council was closely correlated with age. One of the important functions of the council was to adjudicate land disputes that arose between the various kindreds of the island. A *kindred* was a group "reckoning descent and inheriting property from a common ancestor" (MacGregor 1937: 46). The eldest male of the kindred was steward of its holdings and prime director of its affairs, and it was this individual who represented the group in the island council. The eldest woman of the kindred was also an important political figure for she remained on kindred lands throughout her life, whereas the male steward left the holdings when he took up residence with his wife after marriage.

As kindreds grew in membership fissioning commonly occurred and land holdings were correspondingly subdivided. Even when land was reallocated for some other reason new kindreds "form in the succeeding generations, each based on the ownership and inheritance of one of the new land divisions" (MacGregor 1937: 47). Land was, according to MacGregor, "the

chief wealth and dominant interest of the Tokelau native"
(p. 53).

The island council could impose taboos on land. This was
done so that exploitation of coconut groves occurred in rotation.
Individual kindred heads presumably could further regulate
exploitation of those lands under their control. As well as coconuts, *Cordia subcordata (kanava)* timber was a scarce resource
that was closely controlled, since it was used in canoe construction. *Kanava* trees could not be cut without kindred permission. Atafu atoll had more of these trees than the other two
atolls in aboriginal times and occasionally exported them to
Fakaofo and Nukunonu in trade or gift exchanges. The chiefs
of all three atolls also were able to control the exploitation and
distribution of marine resources.

Traditional histories relate that the residents of Fakaofo at
one point defeated Nukunonu and Atafu in warfare. The chief
of Fakaofo then established and assumed the office of paramount chief of the Tokelaus. He first extended a taboo from his
island to the *kanava* trees of the outlying atolls so that *Cordia*
could not be harvested until the proper emissary arrived from
Fakaofo with permission to do so. On Nukunonu he further
imposed a tax of coconuts which had to be sent to Fakaofo, and
apparently this action, combined with the earlier depredations
of warfare, led to starvation among the Nukunonu inhabitants.
Nukunonuans and Atafuans were also obligated to send offerings to the Tui Tokelau, a god on Fakaofo who controlled rainfall and yields of fish and coconuts. The Nukunonuans found
under these circumstances that they could only survive by stealing from the lands confiscated by the Fakaofo victors. Eventually many of the Nukunonuans abandoned their atoll and
moved to Fakaofo itself or sailed to the Ellice Islands.

The population density and political status of particular atolls
within the group waxed and waned through time. The power
of Fakaofo decreased when the atoll suffered severe depopulation in 1846 following a tropical storm. Most of the coconut
trees were destroyed by the strong winds and a large percentage of the population was forced to set off in canoes for the
neighboring atolls in order to avoid starvation, but enroute they
were dispersed by adverse winds. The population of the atoll
apparently fell from a high of 800 to 1000 in 1841 to less than

200 by 1868, partly as a result of this storm, but just as significantly because foreign contact then intervened in a previously
autonomous system. For these islands it took the form of slave
raiding by Peruvians (Hooper and Huntsman 1973: 372).

TUAMOTU ISLANDS

The Tuamotu archipelago is one of the most extensive
coral island chains of the Pacific (Map 11). Population estimates
and adaptation patterns during traditional times are less well
known for this group than for most other areas of the Pacific,
primarily because the archipelago was disrupted so early by
European intervention.

The Tuamotu region is one of the drier of the Pacific, averaging 45 to 60 inches of rain per year, an amount sufficient to
support approximately 30 species of plants and trees in pre-
European times. In 1863 the population of the archipelago was
approximately 6500; it dropped to a low of 4200 in 1926 and
slowly recovered to 6700 by 1951. It has remained at essentially
the same level since then. The population density of the archipelago, with a total land area of 319 square miles, is the
lowest of any area considered in this book, averaging approximately 20 individuals per square mile. Raroia atoll, one of the
most extensively studied of the group, has a land area of 8
square miles and a population of about 160, which makes it
typical for the archipelago. Most of the atolls supported communities with total populations of 100 to 200 individuals. Low
rainfall, which limited agricultural production, undoubtedly
played a major role in keeping densities low in pre-European
times. And today the ease of migration to neighboring high
islands in the Society chain helps to maintain a low density
figure.

The Tuamotus, although outside the hurricane belt of the
south Pacific, occasionally are struck by severe storms. Four of
the most serious swept through the area in 1825, 1877, 1878,
and 1903. The 1878 storm killed 117 residents in Kaukura,
while the 1903 storm killed a total of 517 from several of the
central atolls of the chain (Danielsson 1956: 25–26).

Pandanus was the most important traditional cultivar. Coconuts, Colocasia, arrowroot, and Alocasia (a late introduction)

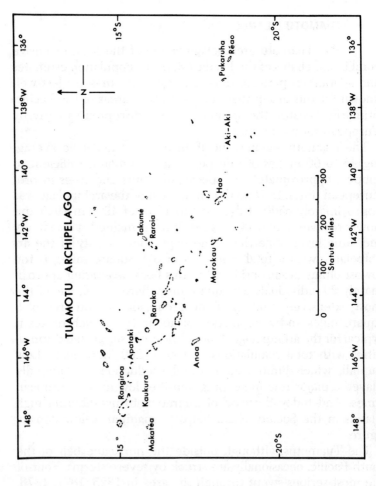

Map 11 Tuamotu Archipelago

TUAMOTU ARCHIPELAGO

15°S

20°S

136°

138°W

140°

142°W

144°

146°W

148°

Pukaruha
Réao

Aki-Aki

Hao

Takumé
Raroia

Marokau

Raraka

Apataki

Anaa

Rangiroa

Kaukura

Makatéa

N

0   100   200   300
Statute Miles

were also important subsistence foods. The pig, dog, and
chicken were absent in precontact times. Fish were abundant
in reef areas and sea turtles a delicacy. In 1842 Lucett (as
quoted by Danielsson) noted that "the natives live principally
on fish and the fruit of the pandanus *(fara)*" (1956: 55).

The Tuamotuans reportedly were accomplished voyagers.
According to folk histories the various atolls of the chain were
originally settled from at least three different areas: the western
atolls from the region of Tahiti, the northeastern atolls possibly
from the Marquesas, and at least some of the southeastern atolls
from Mangareva. In 1837 one observer characterized the Tuamotuans as the "hardiest sailors . . . using their large canoes . . .
covering a distance of several degrees" (Danielsson 1956: 49).
Even in traditional times, then, interisland mobility was common to many of the atolls. Apparently much of this movement
was stimulated by desires to engage in trade or obtain and
secure additional productive land. Interisland social and economic ties were established that linked neighboring islands and
atoll clusters. According to Bengt Danielsson, Raroia and
Takumé formed "one nation" as did Napuka–Tepoto, Takaroa–
Takapoto, and Hao–Amanu. Paul Ottino also identified a larger
interisland cluster in the northwest that included Rangiroa,
Makatea, Tikehau, Matahivi, 'Arutua, Apataki, Kaukura, and
Niau, a grouping that remained important until the 1850s
(1972: 1). Sachiko Hatanaka noted the interdependence of
Pukarua and Reao among the southeastern atolls of the chain.

Localized bilateral (ambilineal) descent groups *('ati)* were
the landholding units of the Tuamotus. Residences were dispersed and postmarital place of residence for a couple depended on land allocations within their respective *'ati.* The
bilateral nature of claiming membership in a descent group
meant that one potentially could opt for membership in more
than one *'ati.* One's active membership, consequently, depended on individual and collective needs, and, if these
changed through time, one could change residence and *'ati*
affiliation. Ottino believed much of this movement grew out of
a need "to maintain the demographical strength . . . at a satisfac-
tory level, together with an appropriate sex ratio" (1967: 476).
Various methods were used to achieve these objectives, including "transfer of descent, exchange of wives . . . and a frequent

resort to adoption. . . ." In Rangiroan society Ottino found that most marriages involved spouses from distant locations—distance in the context of a bilateral society meant less likelihood there would be recognized blood ties between the couple. It also meant that such marriages enlarged land access and claims for both individuals and their kinsmen. On Raroia Danielsson also found that interatoll adoption with residents of Takumé similarly extended land claims and contributed to population mobility between the two atolls.

A high degree of population mobility seems especially well adapted to the aboriginal realities of the Tuamotus, a reality where food shortages, raiding, and warfare were ever-present threats. The dispersed nature of precontact settlement patterns apparently was related to a fear of raiding and the low yields of these water-short islands (Danielsson 1956: 45; Ottino 1967: 475). The alliances formed through marriage and shifting emphases in descent could be utilized both for economic and for defensive purposes.

Pandanus was the most important food of the Tuamotus. It is the most hardy of coral island tree crops and was harvested from August to December. What little taro (Cyrtosperma, Alocasia) there was, was cultivated in small, laboriously excavated pits. Consequently, pandanus and fish, often shellfish, formed the bulk of the diet, and in the period from January to July shortages could sometimes be acute. In 1879 Fierens (quoted by Danielsson) stated the Tuamotuans ". . . are often forced to lie down and hug their bellies in order to alleviate the hunger pains" (1956: 56). Surprisingly, coconut trees were scarce throughout most of the atolls until the late eighteenth century. In 1844 Lucett noted only two coconut trees on Akiaki and for the time this seems typical of most of the atolls of the group (Danielsson 1956: 56). Danielsson proposed two primary reasons for the scarcity: (1) trees were cut down so their cores could be presented as offerings during funeral ceremonies, and (2) victorious raiders purposely destroyed the trees of the defeated as part of the frequent warfare that characterized inter-island affairs. Ottino has proposed a third reason, the fact that residents who feared raiding from stronger neighbors did not plant coconut trees on their island for fear their presence would attract raiders. All of these facts contributed to a self-perpetuating pattern limiting coconut plantings and contributing to chronic food shortages and a pattern of persistent interatoll warfare.

In the 1840s the atoll of 'Ana'a, which was one of the richer and the most densely settled of the Tuamotus, was infamous among its neighbors as the home of raiders who through force of arms extended their political control over much of the archipelago, killing or driving other western Tuamotu inhabitants from their own islands. The 'Ana'ans systematically destroyed the coconut trees of the conquered atolls and consequently only their own atoll was densely planted with them.

The character of interisland relations changed significantly in the mid-1800s with the introduction of Christianity and the expansion of Tahitian political hegemony into the area. The establishment of secure relations with Tahiti resulted in intra-Tuamotus pacification, increased Tahiti–Tuamotus trade, and provided a population safety-valve whereby Tuamotuans could emigrate to Tahiti.

SUMMARY

A community settled on an island or atoll that is part of a cluster is not restricted by the same problems of isolation as are the single islands, as discussed in chapter 4. The larger ecosystem at least postpones for a longer period of time many of the problems associated with overpopulation. The larger resource base can also mean fewer chances of extreme fluctuations of resources and hence can result in greater stability of production for a larger population over a longer period of time. It is more frequently the case, however, that the geographical separation of cluster islands encourages the formation of separate communities with separate identities. This fact may intensify competition for resources when population numbers begin to press on the carrying capacity of the system. On the proposed continuum of coral island ecosystems the cluster is, by definition, similar to the isolate in one fundamental way; that is, in the area of overall productivity. All of the islands of the cluster are producing essentially the same things and possess the same limitations. It follows, then, that there will be some similarities in cultural responses, and this seems especially true in the area of competition. In the isolate setting competition for access to resources often led to internal feuding and intraisland warfare. In the cluster setting competition could lead to larger scale raiding and interisland warfare.

The Manihiki–Rakahanga cluster, at least in its precontact form, bore similarities to an isolate community writ large. The population was settled in a single community and the solidarity of this unit was maintained and supported by a pattern of adaptation that depended on cyclical exploitation of the resources of the two atolls. This was an option basically similar to the tabooed lands and reserve lands strategies of Tongareva and Pukapuka. There were several advantages to the scheme in the cluster setting, however, that were absent in the context of an isolated island. Foremost among these was the fact that no guard system was necessary to protect "reserve" lands. The opportunities for theft were far less in the Manihiki–Rakahanga case than on Pukapuka or Tongareva because the reserve lands were always on the opposite atoll from that of the community's residence. This fact not only relieved manpower, but it undoubtedly reduced intracommunity suspicions and the divisiveness that would follow from such accusations. The fact that the total population moved from one atoll to the other at essentially the same time also would serve to promote a degree of community cooperation. This pattern of exploitation was one step beyond that of the Pukapukans who, periodically, in traditional times, travelled to Nassau to exploit that island's resources. The Pukapukans, however, did not incorporate Nassau as an important part of their ecosystem until postcontact times.

All three atolls of the Tokelau cluster periodically supported permanent communities. Interatoll raiding and warfare apparently became characteristic of the area. Success in raiding or conquest by the residents of one atoll gave access to the resources of another. The victors might annihilate all residents or drive off most of them and extract a periodic tax from those who survived. Subsequently, the conquered atoll was often resettled by colonists from the victorious community. There followed a period of cooperation and exchange during which the daughter-community, if such were established, interacted with the mother-community essentially along kinship lines. If new colonists were not involved, the subjugated islanders were ranked below the victors and taxed accordingly. In time both such communities might break away as independent entities and eventually challenge the social ranking.

The islands of the Tuamotuan cluster appear to have evolved along similar lines. Subsistence production was severely restricted in this archipelago because of environmental limitations, and, consequently, groupings of two or three atolls formed interacting clusters within which personnel and goods were exchanged. Competition for resources became severe and commonly developed into warfare between neighboring clusters. Here, too, populations were annihilated or dispersed as a means of eliminating potential or real threats, and lands distributed or resettled as necessary.

In the Gilbert Islands of Micronesia Makin and Butaritari formed another compact cluster that might be mentioned at this point. Land was controlled by bilateral ramages and membership in the ramage was traced from a founding "owner" of an estate. The operative ramage at any point in time "was composed of those of his descendants who held title to a bed in his Cyrtosperma garden" (Lambert 1971: 149). Movement between the two atolls was common, so much so that some 10 percent of the adults were married to individuals of the opposite atoll. Consequently, many individuals had land claims of one or another type on both atolls. This cluster was under the political control of a single paramount chief. There were three status levels in the society: chiefs, aristocrats, and commoners. The first was composed of the paramount chief and his siblings (who were potential claimants to the office), while the second was made up of the descendants of siblings of previous chiefs. Commoners were obligated to make periodic gifts of Cyrtosperma to a chief when he visited their village. The chief could confiscate abandoned lands and redistribute them, thus guaranteeing maximum productivity.

Further south in the Gilbert chain, in early postcontact times, the chief of Abemama extended his authority to include the atolls of Kuria and Aranuka in a single political system. Previous to this, although interisland travel was never as common as in the neighboring Carolines and Marshalls, raiding between the islands seems to have been frequent. The Gilbertese, in fact, had developed elaborate offensive and defensive battle paraphernalia of sharks' teeth spears and woven coconut sennit armor. Survival in the drier central and southern Gilberts was, in any case, more precarious. Besides feuding and warfare, abortion and infanticide also served to reduce population numbers.

In the Tuamotus localized warring clusters also were drawn together into tighter political units, but this was after the intervention of Tahitian power. With centralization of authority and intensification of status ranking, all of these clusters began to depend more on cooperation and exchange for survival and less on raiding and warfare.

The outstanding variables of cluster adaptations, then, might be diagrammed as in Figure 6. The proximity of coral islands permits a number of options that are extensions of loop 3 of Figure 4. In the early period of occupation there is the probability that access to additional land accommodated an expanding population for a longer period of time than was the case for an isolate. If the communities cooperate, the resulting system may be as the models of Manihiki–Rakahanga or Raroia–Takumé.

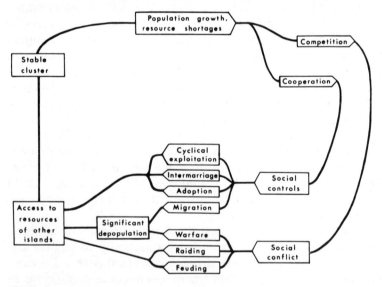

Figure 6 Simplified cluster system diagram. The diagram includes the main variables that tend to alter or maintain a stable cluster community (see text for detailed discussion).

These cooperative arrangements eventually incorporated cultural patterns of intermarriage, adoption, and cyclical migration to exploit the available resources. Social controls were primarily oriented towards redistribution of populations rather than towards limitations in numbers, as was the case among coral isolates. The potentials of the larger ecosystem resulted in stable communities for a longer period of time than was possible in the context of a single coral island.

In time population pressures could lead to conflict that overshadowed cooperation. The alliances in all but the smallest groupings of atolls were fragile, especially so in those areas where there was a chronic scarcity of resources. Raiding and warfare served to reduce populations (those who were actually killed in fighting and those, as in the Tuamotus, who died of starvation that followed destruction of their resources), eliminate competitors, give access to larger resource areas, and provide new areas for subsequent colonization (if the previously resident population was annihilated or dispersed). Population and resource inequities were reduced in each of these cases and a period of community stability followed, at least until resource shortages again reached a critical point.

Centralization of political authority, as apparently was developing in some of these areas, along with patterned economic exchange, provided options for redistribution of resources that did not depend on raiding and warfare, and these options were more fully developed in the larger and more diversified coral complexes.

Chapter 6

CORAL COMPLEXES

The evoution of the Tuamotus from a number of highly competitive coral clusters into a pacified coral complex occurred when Tahitian society extended its control into the area. Tahiti not only pacified the area but also significantly enlarged the ecosystem of the Tuamotus by providing access to additional resources and the opportunity to emigrate. A similar evolution in form probably occurred among the islands of the western and central Carolines, a coral complex that will be discussed in detail in this chapter.

CENTRAL CAROLINE ISLANDS

The coral islands of the central Caroline complex included Ulithi, Fais, Sorol, Woleai, Eauripik, Faraulep, Ifaluk, Elato, Lamotrek, and Satawal (Map 12). The one volcanic island in the complex was Yap, and consequently within the early literature the total is referred to as the "Yap Empire."

Rainfall is uniformly high throughout the coral islands, exceeding 100 inches per annum. Diversified horticulture, at least in the case of the larger atoll islets, is practiced. Cyrtosperma, Colocasia, Alocasia, and breadfruit (fresh and preserved) are the main staples. On the smaller islets such as Eauripik and Faraulep where taro and breadfruit cultivation is difficult, coconuts

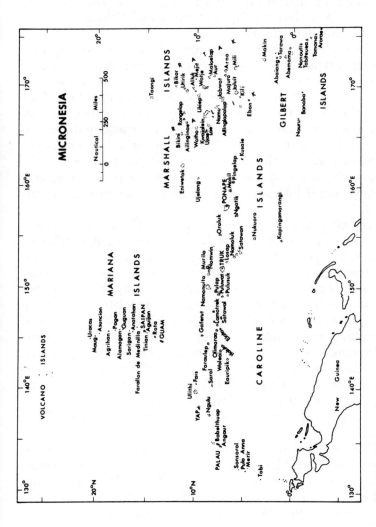

Map 12 Micronesia

increase in dietary importance. On the raised coral island of Fais, sweet potatoes are an important staple. All of these crops are also cultivated on Yap, but in addition, yams *(Dioscorea)* are also raised. In fact on Yap, Dioscorea and Colocasia are the outstanding dietary staples.

The cycles of activity described for Woleai atoll in chapter 3 are fairly typical for all the islands of the complex. Most gardening is the responsibility of women. They cultivate and harvest Cyrtosperma, Colocasia, sweet potatoes, and gather breadfruit with the help of the men who actually climb the trees. Men, on the other hand, are primarily fishermen, exploiting the extensive reef areas of the atolls through a variety of techniques including traps, weirs, nets, spears, and hooks and lines. On those islands that do not have extensive reefs (for example, Satawal and Ifaluk), open ocean trolling for bonito is also important.

The information that is presently available strongly suggests that Yap and the coral outer islands were settled at different times by linguistically distinct populations. Some of the western high islands of Miscronesia apparently were settled by migrants from the Philippines and/or Indonesia as early as 1500 B.C., but 176 A.D. is the oldest archaeological date associated with human settlement on Yap (Gifford and Gifford 1959: 200). The central Caroline coral islands were probably settled at a considerably later date—perhaps around 1000 A.D.—by small groups of settlers moving from east to west. Today the residents of these coral islands speak languages closely related to the vernaculars of Truk and Ponape, all of which are only distantly related to the western Micronesian languages of Yap, Palau, or the Marianas.

The high rainfall and relatively high productivity of the Carolinian coral islands supported some of the densest populations of any of the coral islands of the Pacific. The data of chapter 2, for example, indicate a density generally averaging between 500 and 1000 persons per square mile.

The proximity of the atolls in the central and western Carolines was such that interisland contact and travel was relatively easy and comparatively frequent. Most atolls were less than 100 miles apart. The greatest open ocean distances that had to be crossed were between Woleai and Sorol, a distance of some 200 miles, and the 125 mile voyage from Satawal to Puluwat. These distances were reliably travelled in highly refined sailing craft utilizing relatively sophisticated navigational techniques.

Central Caroline canoes were lateen rigged, double-ended, single outrigger craft. Their hulls consisted of finely hewed keel, strakes and end pieces, all fitted and sewn together. Seams were caulked either with breadfruit tree sap and green coconut husks or with coral lime cement tempered with charcoal. Opposite the single outrigger was a counter-balance platform where goods could be stored or passengers could sit and sleep during travel. When under sail the outrigger was always kept to windward. Consequently, when sailing into the wind, tacking was not achieved by bringing the bow through the eye of the wind, but rather by moving the sail assembly from one end of the craft to the other. This was done by reversing the rake of the ball-and-socket mounted mast. Thus the "bow" became the "stern" (and vice versa) and the craft set off on its new course.

Canoe builders were highly trained craftsmen and their trade was under the protection of specific patron spirits. They utilized precise proportions and measurements in canoe construction, the most important of which were based either on "halving" certain controlling measurements of length or, in a few cases, on anatomical measurements. There were at least twelve different kinds of canoes built, itemized earlier, as two varieties of open ocean sailing craft, two classes of open ocean fishing canoes, two categories of intra-lagoon sailing canoes, five varieties of paddling canoes and one ceremonial craft.

The most highly trained specialists of the central Carolines, however, were the canoe navigators. A qualified Carolinian navigator undertook several years of tutelage from another specialist. He was subject during this time and subsequently to dietary taboos and restrictions on his sexual activities. He was a powerful figure in dealing with the supernatural world, in divination, weather magic, and in some cases sorcery. He was a man who commanded respect, admiration, and sometimes fear.

Central and western Carolinian navigation was based on a celestial compass. The navigator derived the course he would sail from the "star compass" and the particulars of wind direction and set of ocean currents at the time of his voyage. In essence it was a carefully thought-out system of dead reckoning, adapted to the east–west orientation of the island chain. The Carolinian star compass singled out the rising and setting points on the horizon of prominent stars and fixed particular islands at specific points along these paths from every potential point of departure. The master navigator thus memorized a prodigious amount of information in the form of separate star compass charts for every island he intended to visit and these usually totaled a score or more.

The folklore from many of the islands in the region recount earlier times of frequent interisland warfare. Presumably this commonly occurred during periods of dense populations and active competition for resources. Typical of these are tales of an Ifaluk–Woleai war during which a large percentage of the Woleai population was annihilated and several islets of the atoll were resettled by colonists from the victorious Ifaluk. Legends on Lamotrek tell of a similar Lamotrek–Satawal battle in which Satawal was the victor. If these tales were based in fact they refer to periods of interatoll competition that are quite similar to the conditions that prevailed in the Tuamotus, discussed in the previous chapter. But temporally it must have been much earlier, since evidence suggests that for a considerable time before European contact the central and western Caroline coral islands along with Yap, were joined together in a supra-island-level sociopolitical network that tended to minimize conflict and encourage cooperation and exchange.

On most islands, as on Woleai, villages are found strung out along the lagoon or leeward side of an island. Individual dwellings, or small clusters of them, are situated on a parcel of land which usually is identified as the seat of a lineage. There are four important kin groups in these Carolinian communities: the household (based on a descent line), lineage, subclan, and clan. The clan *(gailang)* is a named matrilineal, nonlocalized, and generally exogamous descent group. Postmarital residence in most of the area is matrilocal or uxorilocal (on Ulithi it is patrilocal). The lineage is the basic landholding unit and the residential members constitute the common work group.

Members of different lineages who are able to trace a common relationship consider themselves to be members of the same subclan, and this group effectively is the largest kin group with easily defended inheritance rights. Clan membership gives one a right to expect hospitality and aid from a clansmate when visiting another village or island (if one does not have a closer kinsman resident there); but only in unusual circumstances will common clan membership alone give any one inheritance rights in land belonging to another subclan.

The clans on each island are ranked—some are chiefly and others commoner. The chiefly status of a clan is related to seniority of settlement on each particular island, therefore the chiefly status of a clan on one island does not automatically mean its members will have a like status on any other, although certain clans of ancient origin do control a higher percentage of the chiefly offices of the region.

Every inhabited island is divided into a number of districts (most commonly two or three) and each district is represented in island affairs by a chief who is usually the senior male of the senior lineage of the highest ranked clan of the district. If there is a significant seniority difference between the eldest male and eldest female of the chiefly clan within the district, the woman may be selected by clan members as their chief. In some cases there may also be a paramount chief who has authority over the whole island. This individual, of course, is drawn from the highest ranking clan of the island and this clan may thus fill two political offices; that is, one of the district chieftainships and that of the paramount chief.

Even though all clans and chiefs are ranked it is most common for the chiefs to reach collective decisions in island-wide affairs, often in consultation with the heads of the commoner clans of the island. In day-to-day political affairs, then, personality characteristics may be more important in decision making than actual rank and, if so, a clan head of subordinate status may actually be quite influential. The ranking system embracing the chiefly offices operates so that in island-level affairs there are definite channels of communication and decision making, and this tends both to minimize open conflict and to encourage cooperation. A chief has the authority to organize and initiate district or island-wide activities and ceremonies and, concurrently, has the responsibility to maintain peace and quiet. It is the chief who decides, for example, when communal fishing expeditions are undertaken, when village paths are cleaned and repaired, when a particular ceremony is held, and how long a funeral taboo must last. If someone under his authority breaks the peace or violates a restriction, the chief can impose sanctions on the individual or on the whole population under his jurisdiction. These sanctions most commonly involve restrictions and limitation of standard activities. For example, the chief can forbid drinking of palm wine or dancing, restrict fishing in certain communal fishing areas, or perhaps impose a small fine based on either traditional valuables (such as woven fiber skirts and loin cloths) or, more recently, on money which is obtained from sale of copra.

A chief on most islands also has first-fruits rights in his district. At the beginning of the breadfruit season all landholding groups within a district must offer these fruits to the chief, who redistributes them among all the residents of his district or, in some cases, exchanges them with the chief of the other districts of the island in an island-wide ceremony.

As noted in chapter 2, the central and western Caroline Islands lie within the typhoon belt of the northwestern Pacific. All of the islands of the area periodically have experienced the devastation of serious tropical storms. In fact between 15 and 18 severe storms develop in the greater Micronesian area each year (Wiens 1962: 173). Some of these develop and disintegrate without affecting inhabited islands, but many do cause extensive damage to islands and their inhabitants. In the case of Lamotrek, at the eastern end of the Caroline complex, severe typhoons are known to have struck the atoll in 1815, 1845, 1907, and 1958. In the Woleai–Ifaluk region, near the center of the complex, six severe storms were experienced between 1900 and 1950. At the western end of the chain, Ulithi–Fais have been hit by 5 typhoons over the last 80 years (Lessa 1964: 17). The March 1907 typhoon, mentioned in chapter 3, was one that seems to have affected nearly all of the islands of the central and western Carolines. However, it is more usual for only two or three atolls to be severely damaged by any one storm before it turns north and moves on towards the Philippines or Japan. Quite often, therefore, one atoll or a cluster of closely associated atolls is severely damaged by a storm while the neighboring islands and atolls 50 or more miles away are not affected. This fact, combined with the differential productive potential of the atolls, has encouraged the development of systems of inter-island cooperation and exchange which tend to guarantee survival for the residents of the various islands during these times of stress.

The social and natural environment crucial to central Carolinian adaptation involves alliances at several levels. Three examples are the intra-atoll exchange system (*chúlifeimag*) of Woleai atoll, the interisland "hook" *(hù)* centered on Lamotrek, and in earlier times an overseas exchange system *(sawei)* which tied together all of the inhabited coral islands of the region to Yap.

The *chúlifeimag* of Woleai links the seven inhabited islands of the atoll. These islands are so situated that three are found on the western side of the atoll and four at the eastern end (Map 2). Among the residents of Woleai this separation is spoken of as if the islands were located on separate western and eastern lagoons and the *chúlifeimag* links individual districts or islands of the two lagoons. For example, Sùlywap, an island of the western lagoon, is tied to Ifang district of Falalap Island in the eastern lagoon; Tabwogap district of Wottagai Island of the western lagoon is tied to Lùlipelig, another district of Falalap of the eastern lagoon; and so on, so that all the islands in the west are tied to islands in the east. Periodically gifts of coconuts, breadfruit, or fish are made by one island or district to its partner in the opposite lagoon. The paired districts or islands also jointly control fishing rights over certain reef areas of the atoll. The gifts most commonly are made when one of the districts has a surplus of produce or fish. The *chúlifeimag* thus serves as a means to redistribute goods which are locally and periodically plentiful in a manner that reinforces solidarity between distant parts of the atoll.

There are other less formal exchange patterns within the atoll that serve a similar purpose, both between the islands of a single lagoon and between the islands of the atoll as a whole. The funeral on Wottagai that was described in chapter 3 was one such example. Here the unity among islands of the same lagoon was an accepted reality without a formal named exchange system. Rather the residents accepted the fact that any funeral ceremony which was centered on Wottagai automatically involved Falalus and Sùlywap as well. Individuals on Falalus, Wottagai, and Sùlywap verbalized this when they stated that the people of these islands were "as one."

Further atoll solidarity was manifest in the installation ceremony for a new chief. The unity of the east and west was symbolized through the presentation of a gift of 1000 ripe coconuts to each of the islands of the opposite lagoon attending the installation ceremony. By accepting these coconuts the visitors from the opposite lagoon acknowledge the end of the funeral taboo period for the old chief and the authority of the new chief on his island. All of these patterned exchange systems permit a more even distribution of subsistence goods throughout the atoll.

At the eastern end of the Caroline complex the three islands of Lamotrek, Elato, and Satawal were participants in a more highly ranked interisland and interatoll exchange system (Map 13). Lamotrek is the pivotal island of this group and the highest in rank. The people of Elato and Satawal, through their chiefs until recent times, submitted semi-annual tribute to the paramount chief of Lamotrek, who in turn redistributed the tribute received to all the residents of Lamotrek. This tribute was basic to the "hook" exchange system.

Central Carolinians divided the year into two seasons and once each season the Satawal and Elato people were obligated to send tribute to Lamotrek. During the May to October season the Satawal chief in preparation for this event required each lineage on his island to provide one basket of preserved breadfruit as its share of the tribute payment. The total, which averaged 15 baskets, was then taken to Lamotrek. In the November-to-April season, the Satawal chief similarly assembled 1000 ripe coconuts as tribute. Five sailing canoes were needed on each occasion to transport these tribute payments. Similarly, the chief of Elato once each season (but not necessarily at the same time as his Satawal counterpart) sent three live green sea turtles from his island to Lamotrek as tribute. The Lamotrek chief was not required to make a return presentation to Satawal or Elato. However, if a surplus of fish was available on the island at the time tribute was received, he might choose to do so. But the tribute payments did guarantee that Satawal and Elato, islands of lower status than Lamotrek, had the right to request aid from Lamotrek in times of food shortages. For

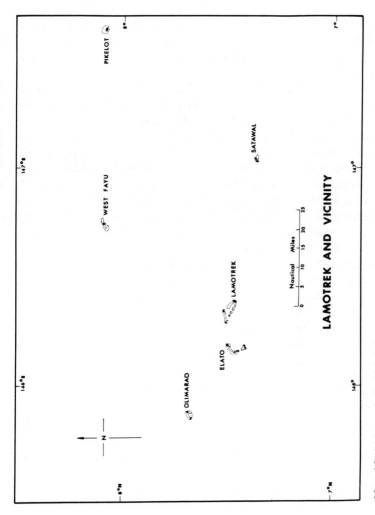

Map 13 Lamotrek and Vicinity

example, after a typhoon in 1958 which struck all three islands, the chief of Satawal requested several thousand ripe coconuts from the chief of Lamotrek. Although Lamotrek also had been severely damaged by the storm the Lamotrek chief agreed to furnish the nuts as well as several subsequent shipments until 1960. Satawal, being a raised coral island, was more dependent on coconuts for food than Lamotrek, the latter having extensive taro fields.

Tribute payments also assured for the residents of Satawal and Elato important rights to exploit several nearby uninhabited islands and reefs that Lamotrek claimed were under her eminent domain. Olimarao, West Fayu, and Pikelot were the most important of these nearby islands. Satawal relied heavily on West Fayu for a large percentage of her sea turtle catch while in earlier times, when the island was more densely settled, Elato residents depended on the additional resources of Olimarao. Recognition of Lamotrek's suzerainty over the uninhabited islands was symbolized in an additional ceremonial presentation made by individuals of Elato and Satawal if they should meet residents of Lamotrek on a visit to any of the three uninhabited islands. On such occasions the Elato or Satawal visitors were obligated to present the Lamotrek voyagers with at least one head from any turtles the former had taken on the island. In summary, Elato and Satawal were tied to Lamotrek by the "hook" and had to convey tribute to this higher ranking island. In return they could freely exploit resource areas claimed by Lamotrek. And more importantly, by virtue of the hook, the three islands were obligated to support each other in times of resource shortages.

The widest exchange system and highest level of unity in the Caroline atoll complex was embodied in the *sawei* overseas exchange system. At its height this system linked all the atolls from Namonuito to Ulithi to specific villages on Yap. Until early in this century, approximately once each year tribute was delivered to Gatchepar and Wanyan villages of Gagil district on Yap by representatives from nearly all the outer islands who travelled to Yap in a fleet of canoes (Lessa 1950; Alkire 1965; 1970). The tribute expedition began on those islands most distant from Yap, with canoes carrying representatives from Namonuito, Pulap, and Pulusuk sailing to Puluwat. At this stop the Puluwat delegate joined them and the fleet moved on first to Satawal and then to Lamotrek. Lamotrek was an important stopover point where representatives from both this island and Elato were waiting to join. After a period of rest and with favorable winds this enlarged fleet set sail for Olimara district on Wottagai Island—the highest ranking *sawei* district of Woleai atoll. Representatives from Ifaluk, Eauripik, and Faraulep, as well as the various districts of Woleai, were assembled at Olimara. This group then left Woleai for Fais where this island's representative was picked up by one of the visiting canoes. The people of Fais were unusual among Caroline Islanders in that they did not possess sailing canoes of their own. After Fais one more stop was made at Mogmog Island in Ulithi atoll before the voyage ended at Gagil, Yap.

At the major stopovers of the voyage the chief of the highest ranking island took charge of the whole fleet. Since the rank of the outer islands generally increased as one approached Yap, the three most important leaders of the expedition successively were the paramount chief of Lamotrek, followed by the chief of Olimara district of Wottagai, Woleai, and finally by the chief of Mogmog, Ulithi, who dealt directly with the Yapese chief when the expedition arrived at Faliso canoe house in Gatchepar village, Yap.

The emissaries from each of the islands carried three categories of gifts which were, respectively, Religious Tribute, Canoe Tribute, and Tribute of the Land. The first two were always in the keeping of the leader of the expedition. Consequently, these kinds of tribute were transferred to different canoes at Lamotrek, Woleai, and Ulithi. When the expedition reached Fais the chief from Olimara, Woleai (who was leader at this point) presented part of the Canoe Tribute to the chief of Fais. In addition, the representatives of Ifaluk, Falalus Island, Woleai and Pigùl district of Wottagai, Woleai, all of whom had important *sawei* ties to Fais, presented the chief of this latter island with a share of their Religious Tribute. The rest of the tribute was carried on to Ulithi with the expedition where the Mogmog chief retained a certain percentage for his island, given by all the other representatives who had direct *sawei* ties to this island. At the end of the voyage on Yap, the Mogmog chief gave the Canoe Tribute and Religious Tribute to the chief of Gatchepar. Then the emissaries of the other islands dispersed in order to visit the dwellings of their specific *sawei* partners, to whom they presented their Land Tribute. These individuals were Yapese lineage heads who claimed ownership of the islands or districts from which the representatives came. Most of the tribute was made up of woven fiber skirts or loincloths, sennit twine, and shell valuables. The coral islanders then waited for a seasonal change of winds before setting sail for their home islands. During this time they were supported by their *sawei* partners. At the time of their departure these Yapese usually presented them with counter-gifts of food and turmeric.

The outer islanders believed that tribute voyages to Yap were necessary, otherwise the Yapese could invoke their superior magic and control of the supernatural to destroy the outer islands with destructive storms and typhoons. The Yapese of Gagil, on the other hand, referred to the outer islanders as their "children" who were allowed to live on and exploit land belonging to their Yapese "fathers," and the tribute payments were symbolic recognition of this fact of ownership.

The overseas exchange system, the hook system, and the Woleai intra-atoll system were similar in structure and function. They all served to link communities on a number of small, dispersed and vulnerable islands situated in a typhoon zone of the western Pacific. These ties permitted members of the ranked societies to move freely between islands and to request and expect aid from any other island within the system in case of disaster and resource shortages. The systems also facilitated "everyday" exchange as well, so that regular and/or predictable localized shortages of food, timber, and other resources and personnel could easily be balanced. The sociopolitical and kinship ties between the islands made it relatively easy for individuals to move from one island to another, if necessary, to overcome the uneven distribution of certain classes of individuals.

One example of this process is illustrated by the frequency of interisland marriages within the Caroline complex. Data from Lamotrek, Elato, and Woleai show that in recent times at least some 25 percent of the marriages on each of these islands were between spouses from different atolls or islands (Table 4). Since divorce and remarriage were common on all three of these atolls until very recently, one finds that the frequency of such "overseas" marriages increased with age. At least some of these marriages were probably arranged to compensate for local problems of sterility. If one compares, in this table, the percentage of childless women on Lamotrek and Elato with the figures for overseas marriages and average frequency of marriage, one sees a clear tendency for the frequency of divorce and remarriage to increase, not only with age, but also as the percentage of childless females increases. The highest frequency is reached among men in the 46–55 year age cohort, who during their lives, on the average, have married six different times. And again on the average, three of these marriages were to women from other islands or atolls. These men were generally marrying women somewhat younger than themselves, probably in the age range of 36–45 years. The fact that sterility is highest among women of this age category suggests a local problem that probably encouraged both divorce and remarriage and seeking out of potential spouses from neighboring island. The figures from Woleai atoll are not as striking in this regard.

Hunt, Kidder, and Schneider (1954: 41) have suggested that anything in excess of 25 percent sterility (childless women) is an abnormally high figure by world standards. Those women 40 to 60 years of age at the time this census was taken were of child bearing age during the latter part of the Japanese administration; a period when military personnel were stationed on many of the islands of the area. Lessa and Myers (1962) believe that veneral disease was widespread on some of the islands of the region at that time and this resulted in increased sterility. The apparently low number of individuals in the 16–25 year age cohort (Table 5), who were children of these women in the 40–60 year categories, may be an obvious consequence of this sterility and also may serve to support this hypothesis.

Venereal disease may not have been as serious a problem on Woleai during these same years as it was on Lamotrek, since all but a handful of the native residents of Woleai left the atoll for Ifaluk during the period of military occupation. There were other factors, as well, that undoubtedly contributed to increasing numbers of inter-island and inter-atoll marriages during the 1930s. Foremost among these was the increasing number of Micronesians who were moving from island to island within the

Table 4 Interisland marriages, childless women, and marriage frequency on Lamotrek (1962) and Woleai (1965)

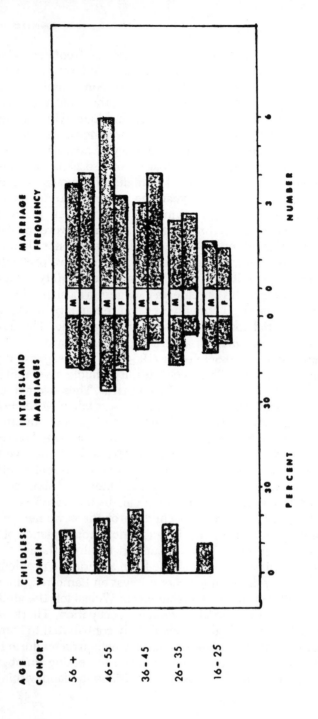

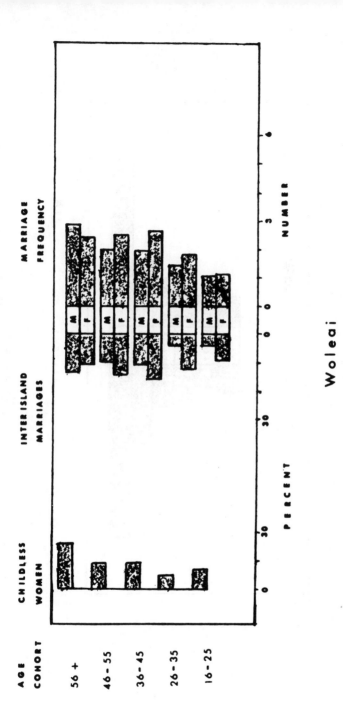

Woleai

Table 5 Population pyramid by age and sex for Woleai (1965) and Lamotrek (1962)

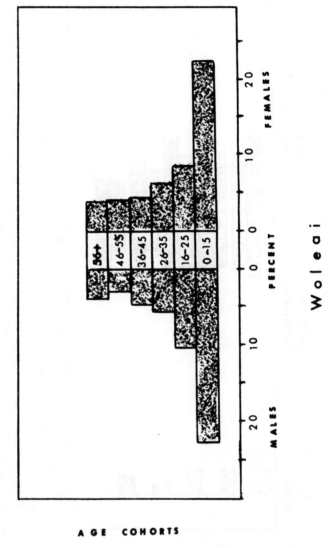

AGE COHORTS

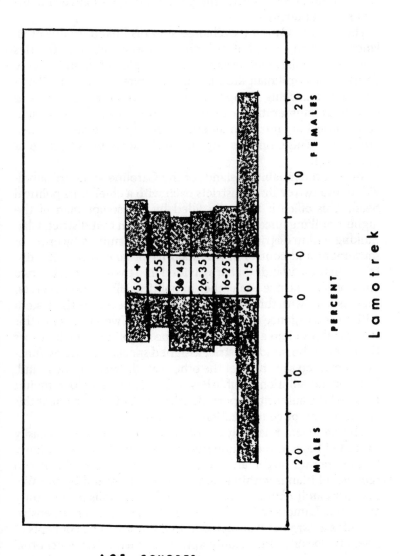

AGE COHORTS

56 + / 46-55 / 36-45 / 26-35 / 16-25 / 0 -15

PERCENT

MALES   FEMALES

20   10   0   0   10   20

Lamotrek

area as employees of either the government or of government-sponsored enterprises.

These three Caroline exchange systems linked groups of islands of varying size, but in each case the structure of the ties was quite similar. One organizing principle common in many domains of Carolinian atoll life incorporates a dualistic "halving" and balancing of oppositions. Such cultural domains as diverse as enumeration, canoe and house building, navigation, and political organization all emphasize dualistic divisions (Alkire 1970). This emphasis appears in the structure of the complex as well.

Most of the inhabited islands of the Caroline atolls are subdivided into two or three districts each with a chief as its political head. This office is normally filled by the senior man of the highest ranking lineage of the ranking clan in that district. Clan ranking within districts was apparently determined by order of settlement and control of the majority of land within the district. On those islands that are divided into two districts, the two chiefs easily balance each other in political affairs. However, on those islands with three districts an imbalance enters the system with the emergence of three chiefly offices. Two solutions to this structural problem are common in the Carolines. The first sees the chief of the middle district assigned special mediating functions between the chiefs of the other two districts on the island. The second solution establishes a fourth office of paramount chief, whose authority supersedes that of all others. In effect this option is one of centralization of power.

This basic and relatively simple political structure was easily extended beyond the boundaries of a single island community to incorporate larger and larger numbers of participants; to include all islands within a large atoll as illustrated by the Woleai intra-atoll *chúlifeimag;* to a number of atolls in proximity as in the Lamotrek "hook"; or to all islands of an extensive complex as large as that included in the *sawei.* The concepts of lineality, locality, and duality appear as part of the conceptual order in each case. In the *chúlifeimag* of Woleai, goods flow along definite lines to specific points in such a way as always to link opposing halves of the atoll. Within the hook, Lamotrek stands first between Elato and Satawal and second between both of these islands and the neighboring uninhabited resource islands. Finally, the structure of the *sawei* conceives of Ulithi, the highest ranking coral atoll of the complex, as mediating between Yap and "the Woleai"—that is, between all of the other outer islands. Further, when the system was viewed from the perspective of Woleai, a similar opposition was verbalized as the participants spoke of Olimara (Woleai) lying between the halves of "Greater Lamotrek" *(Lamotrekalaplap)* to the east, and Ulithi-Fais to the west.

These principles of organization are eminently suited to the environmental setting in which the people of the coral islands of the Carolines found themselves, but are not necessarily direct outgrowths of that environment since some of these organizing principles apparently have historical antecedents in Southeast Asia (Alkire 1972b). Nevertheless, within the Carolines survival depended on maintaining contact between a large number of discrete islands and atolls, and the basic structure of this local organization was easily expanded to permit orderly exchange and cooperation in utilization of resources by larger groupings of islands.

MARSHALL ISLANDS

Relatively sophisticated navigational knowledge and interisland sailing skills were obviously required in the development of a coral island sociopolitical complex. The Marshall Islands archipelago was a second area in the Pacific where such skills were found, along with the two prerequisites of island diversity and proximity.

Ratak and Ralik are the two parallel chains of this archipelago and together they include 29 atolls and 5 raised coral islands (Map 11). The total land area involved is only 74 square miles with a current average population density of 270 persons per square mile. There are no volcanic islands in the Marshalls, but there is a degree of habitat diversity within the archipelago related to variations in atoll size and amount of rainfall. Both of these variables fundamentally influence horticultural and marine productivity. The atoll islets of the Marshalls are similar to those of the Carolines but are often considerably larger. Some islets stretch along the reef for 10 or perhaps 20 miles. Consequently, on atolls of this size it more frequently happens that a

single island will support several dispersed and relatively autonomous villages. Furthermore, there is a significant difference in
rainfall between the drier northern islands of each chain and
the wetter southern islands. The statistics cited in chapter 2
verify this. Bikini in the north, for example, receives 60 inches
per year compared to the 160 inches that annually fall on Arno
in the south. The northern inhabitants, then, must depend on
the hardier crops of coconuts, pandanus, and arrowroot for
subsistence, while in the south breadfruit and taro are more
important. The basic land division of the Marshalls was called
a *wato*, which was a strip that runs the width of an islet from
the lagoon to the ocean. Traditionally, one or more of these
strips was held and administered as an estate by a particular
matrilineage *(bwij)* or descent line of the society. The men of
the residence planted crops, harvested, and fished along the
reef and in the lagoon. This meant that in the northern islands
late in the year the men spent a large part of their time gathering, preparing, and preserving pandanus while in the southern
islands, where breadfruit was so important, most other activities
were postponed during the annual harvest while this crop was
prepared for preservation.

The lineage head was steward of the lineage landholdings.
Ordinary lineage members passed a portion of their produce to
this head, some of which he kept and some of which he passed
on to higher ranking political figures who held residual rights
in, or eminent domain over, all lands.

Interisland travel in the Marshalls was probably as frequent
as that described for the central and western Carolines. The
principles of Marshallese navigation were somewhat different.
They emphasized techniques of interpretation and analysis of
currents and waves rather than celestial observations and the
development of a star compass (Davenport 1960). Most voyaging in the Marshalls was between islands that lay in the same
chain and hence involved north–south travel in either Ralik or
Ratak. Both of these chains lie at right angles to the prevailing
northeast trade winds and the easterly sea swell that is carried
before the winds. The closely spaced islands and reefs of the
archipelago consequently interrupt the smooth transit of the
swell, deflecting waves and currents in relatively predictable
and constant patterns. The basis of traditional Marshallese navi-

gation focused on interpreting these patterns. A trâined navigator was able to fix his location when out of sight of land by observing the surrounding wave patterns and conceptually tracing the origins of the pattern back to a known reef or island of the archipelago.

The sailing canoes of the Marshalls were among the most technically advanced of the Pacific. They incorporated all of the features of Carolinian canoes that were previously discussed, but in addition they were generally larger, faster, and probably more stable. These craft, in combination with a detailed knowledge of local sea conditions, permitted the Marshallese to establish and maintain frequent contact with the various communities throughout the area and to transport more people, more easily, between them. This ease of interisland travel and communication had political ramifications.

The chief of Ailinglapalap was able to extend his control over most of Ralik with the exception of Eniwetok and Ujelang. Periodically thereafter this chief and his successors sailed in circuit to these islands with his retainers to collect tribute. The chain subsequently was divided into two districts; one included Namu and the islands to the north, and the other Jabwol, Ailinglapalap, and the islands to the south. Although all these islands were "owned" by the paramount chief, he rarely called at those further north than Kwajalein and Ujae; largely because of their isolation and rainfall—limited resources—they were too impoverished to provide any worthwhile tribute. This complex differed from that of the central Caroline Islands in several ways. Politically, it was more highly centralized. The paramount chief maintained his control, in part, by visiting his subject islands to collect tribute. His authority was probably derived more directly from political force. The unity of the system nevertheless permitted a wider exchange of economic goods and personnel, both in times of drought in the north, or following storm damage in the south.

Ratak was similarly organized but less centralized. This chain was never unified under a single paramount chief, although the chief of Maloelap was able to put all the islands to the north with the exception of Mejit under his control. Eventually, however, Majuro and Arno broke away from this alliance and reestablished their independent political status. The Ralik and Ratak alliances both were in a state of flux and varied in size as local chiefs tested their own strength vis-à-vis that of the paramount chief. This tendency towards fission was one thing that encouraged the paramount chief to move his residence from island to island to make his control clearly visible to the local district chiefs. Another reason for these moves was that the chief and his entourage were a resource drain on the atoll where they resided. The Yapese "overlords" of the Caroline complex resided in a richer and more secure setting and saw no advantage to residing on the other islands of the complex.

SUMMARY

The ecosystems of the two coral complexes discussed each involved island groupings with a significant degree of internal variation. The Carolinian complex encompassed a large number of small and moderately sized atolls, two raised coral islands, and the volcanic Yap Island. Among these islands exists a degree of differential productivity related to size, topography, and situation. Satawal, for example, because of elevation and relative breadth, has a larger number of breadfruit trees than neighboring Lamotrek. Lamotrek, on the other hand, with a lower average elevation and extensive interior swamps, produces more Cyrtosperma, Colocasia, and tobacco. Many of the voyages between the two islands were undertaken to obtain these differentially available resources. Similarly, turtle and tradacna shell belts produced on Eauripik found their way to Woleai, Ifaluk, and the other islands of the complex as far as Yap. In fact several varieties of Yapese valuables, or so-called money, originated in the outer islands, including banana fiber cloth (called *mbuc* in Yapese) and mother-of-pearl shells (*yar*).

The east-west orientation of the chain within the typhoon belt of the western Pacific meant that single islands or a number of islands might be severely damaged by passing storms. Survival of the affected population could easily become dependent on the resources of neighboring unaffected communities. In this context the emphasis in a systems diagram such as that of Figure 7 is on cooperation rather than competition. A cooperative

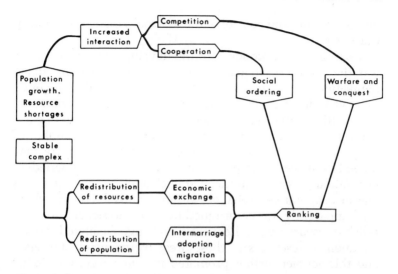

Figure 7 Simplified complex system diagram. The diagram includes those variables that contribute to maintaining and altering stability in a coral complex community (see text for detailed discussion).

exchange system would appear to be a better "insurance policy" than a pattern of competitive raiding and feuding, since a community struck by a typhoon would not be in a strong position to mount a successful raid on the resources of a neighboring island. Furthermore, if raiding and feuding were the predominant patterns, there would always be the danger that certain islands periodically would be stripped of their resources and residents, essentially taking such areas out of production for a period of time. The unpredictability of typhoons is such that this might occur at the very time when the resources of these islands were most needed.

Differential productivity was also a feature of the Marshalls complex. In this instance the wetter and richer southern islands contrasted with the drier and more marginal northern ones. Typhoons were less frequent in this archipelago and the interisland ties that were characteristic of the complex apparently were developed by political pressure and military force. The proximity of the islands seemingly contributed to the ease with which this was possible and to the more centralized character of the complex. Concomitantly, there was more internal jockeying for position and control in the Marshalls than in the central Carolines.

A significant consequence of the development of a complex was the possiblity of maintaining a denser and more stable population. The actual steps involved in its evolution might be somewhat different, involving varying degrees of cooperation, competition, force, and conflict. The end results were to guarantee access to a larger resource base for a larger number of people. In the case of the Carolinian complex warfare may indeed have been an important consideration during periods of population pressure, but the overall character of the *sawei* was one of cooperative exchange within a ranked system, where rank apparently was determined by access to richer and more reliable resource areas. Economic exchange facilitated the distribution of resources to those areas experiencing shortages, and this contact further promoted intermarriage, interisland adoption and interisland migration that shifted personnel to those areas with potential or real resource surpluses.

In the Marshalls complex resource shortages initially resulted in competition, conflict, and warfare. A shifting hierarchical ranking emerged that promoted interisland exchanges and again redistribution of resources and population resulted. Ranking and status differentiation were important to both of these systems (Figure 7) and served to centralize control, minimize competition, and establish well defined channels of interaction that facilitated redistribution of goods and personnel.

Several other examples of coral complexes could be identified and discussed, especially in the region of Melanesia. The works of Thompson (1949, 1970) and Davenport (1975) suggest that networks of coral islands in the vicinity of Fiji and the Santa Cruz Islands, respectively, possess many of the characteristics of complexes. Detailed consideration of either of these areas, however, would take us beyond the stated Micronesia-Polynesia focus of this book.

Chapter 7

EMERGING STRUCTURES

Modern transportation and communication have lessened the importance of isolation as an adaptive variable for the coral island areas of the Pacific. Islands that once were almost totally isolated from their neighbors now may have frequent contact not only with such neighbors, but also with locales as distant as North America, Japan, and Australasia.

In most of the Pacific reliable and scheduled transportation was initially sponsored or subsidized by European, American, or Asian metropolitan powers who were primarily interested in developing the copra trade. Consequently, from the mid-nineteenth century to the present the coral islands of the Pacific have become more and more closely tied to world economic conditions.

At various times over the last 100 years colonial governments and missionary groups have encouraged the planting of additional coconuts in nearly every area of Micronesia and Polynesia. On many islands this not only resulted in the hoped-for export of copra, but also in local dietary changes. In some cases, as in the Tuamotus, increased plantings provided a reliable and much needed food crop where previously only a marginal existence was possible. In other cases, as in the Marshalls, increased plantings led to decreased consumption of other traditional staples, such as pandanus, since the trees of the latter were removed to allow for more extensive plantings of coconuts. And in yet other instances the result was one of decreased consumption of all traditional foods, the coconut included, in favor of increased consumption of imported foodstuffs, purchased with the returns from copra sales. The islands of this last category are the ones most seriously affected by the vagaries and fluctuations of world markets. A very few coral islands possessed other resources that were of value to metropolitan powers. The phosphate deposits of Nauru and Banaba are such examples.

The regular shipping schedules that were instituted to even the most remote of Pacific coral islands were continued in order to obtain these resources and to gain certain strategic advantages in the area. The cultural changes that followed have been many. Nauru, once an isolate, is now an independent nation financed by phosphate royalties. The 4000 people of the island now own both a shipping company and an airline that provide biweekly contacts with Japan, Australia, and other areas of the Pacific. Kapingamarangi, Niue, Tongareva, and Pukapuka, similarly, are no longer isolated although contact with the outside world is far less extensive and frequent. Nevertheless, in all of these cases modern transportation and communication have significantly altered the isolate ecosystem by introducing the option of emigration as a real cultural choice. In precontact times this was an option only possible to residents of clusters and complexes. All of the isolates discussed in this book currently have emigration outlets, and, in some cases, large numbers of individuals have in fact established "daughter communities" on relatively distant high islands.

A permanent Kapingamarangi community named Porakiet has grown up on Ponape, the nearest high island to the atoll, although it lies nearly 500 miles away. This community was first established in 1919 on a piece of land leased from the Japanese colonial administration. The land thus obtained was originally needed to accommodate some 40 to 45 Kapingamarangi contract laborers and their families who worked for a Japanese company on Ponape. But the 1916–1918 drought and famine encouraged additional emigration as "individuals and their families were offered the chance to go to Ponape and get work and wages as an alternative to starving at home" (Lieber 1968:

7). In subsequent years rapid population growth on Kapin-gamarangi "has been mitigated by the ability of Porakiet to absorb the excess population ..." (Lieber 1968: 89). The Porakiet community retained a separate identity and in its initial years was socially isolated from surrounding Ponapean communities. The initial settlers, who were transient laborers and those seeking relief from the food shortages of their own island, had no intention of spending the rest of their lives on Ponape, consequently they saw no need to establish extracommunity social contacts. In recent years, however, many in Porakiet have accepted Ponape as their permanent place of residence, and social interaction with Ponapeans has increased. Initially, the community experienced a relatively high degree of lawlessness and drunkeness among younger residents who upon arrival felt free and far removed from traditional sanctions, chiefs, and kinsmen. Subsequently, such antisocial conduct was brought under effective control when an internal governing structure was agreed to by the residents.

Among the other isolates similar emigration possibilities have opened up. The Pukapukans in recent years have increased their reliance on Nassau to full "cluster proportions." These islanders fully realized in the early 1950s that their own atoll could not accommodate an ever-expanding population. In 1951 they purchased Nassau from the New Zealand government, in part to legitimize a traditional claim, and in part to anticipate increasing resource needs. Within a few years a permanent colony of Pukapukans was established on Nassau, and today that community has grown to 170 permanent residents. Pukapuka itself supports an additional 760 people, while yet others have emigrated to Rarotonga and New Zealand. Julia Hecht, in fact, has stated that as many Pukapukans now live in New Zealand as remain in their home islands (Percival 1974: 61).

Rarotonga and New Zealand are also the main destinations for people emigrating from the other islands of the Northern Cooks and from Niue. Consequently, all of the former isolate communities have emigration opportunities and have established external ties that serve as safety valves for overpopulation and that permit new adaptive choices.

Two other features of the traditional isolate sociocultural system that have been most directly affected by these modern events are the patterns of warfare and political authority. All coral isolate communities have been pacified either directly by the intervention of a metropolitan power or indirectly as the result of easing population pressures. Initially, introduced diseases and slave raiding resulted in significant depopulation, while subsequently emigration has similar consequences. Political authority, especially the definition of chiefly powers, has also been altered. In some cases metropolitan controlled colonial administrations stripped local chiefs of their authority; in other cases the authority of chiefs has withered as those under them have seen new options or gained access to resources outside the traditional system. For example, those individuals who believe they are unjustly affected by a chief's decision may now choose to leave the island and establish themselves elsewhere. Other residents may circumvent the authority of a chief, an option made possible by the returns from the copra trade. This money generally has reduced the chief's authority as a redistributive figure. The money obtained from copra sales is often conceived of as lying outside the traditional system and consequently beyond traditional controls.

The advent of the copra trade, modern transport, and communication have also altered the dimensions of coral cluster and complex ecosystems. Interisland canoe travel, so basic to cluster and complex adaptations, has decreased or disappeared in most areas and has been replaced by commercial transport. Typical of this development is the situation in the Tuamotus, where Danielsson (1956: 132) noted that there were only a very few boats and canoes on Raroia seaworthy enough to make the trip to Takumé and none were capable of sailing to any more distant island or atoll. This is the state of affairs in an area that was once renowed for its interisland navigators. At the same time, some 38 trading vessels called at Raroia in 1950. The communication networks and patterns of interdependence that have resulted from this contact may be quite different from that developed in traditional times. The routing of steamships and trading vessels may, in fact, make it more easy to visit distant ports on the main islands of the various archipelagoes than to visit nearby coral island neighbors.

The coral complex of the central Carolines has experienced significant alteration in form owing to similar external influences. Long distance interisland canoe travel began to decrease during the German period of administration in Micronesia (1899–1914). Both the Germans and their colonial successors, the Japanese, discouraged such voyaging, not only because of the dangers inherent in such travel and the expenses associated with searches for lost canoes and repatriation of shipwrecked voyagers who were washed ashore at distant locales, but also, some believe, because of the lost revenues suffered by their steamship companies. Islanders who could not travel by canoe between islands would have to purchase passage on such steamships if they wished to continue visiting neighbors. Furthermore the presence of the Germans and later the Japanese and Americans in the central Carolines meant that wide-ranging interisland voyages became less necessary as a means to redistribute goods since these colonial powers were in a position to offer and guarantee emergency relief to typhoon stricken islands more efficiently than was possible through the traditional *sawei*. Nevertheless in much of this area the memory of the *sawei* and island interdependence is still strong and given the right set of circumstances this memory can give rise to a revitalization of some aspects of the old patterns. A former Satawal–Saipan connection is illustrative of this fact.

At the height of Carolinian voyaging, trips were undertaken not only among *sáwei* islands as far away as Yap, but also from Satawal, Lamotrek, and Woleai to Guam and Saipan in the Mariana Islands. There is evidence that suggests that the Carolinians first came into contact with the Spanish and gained access to European trade goods, especially iron, during one of their annual voyages to the Marianas (Kotzebue 1821, 3: 233 ff.). Saipan became even more important to these Carolinians following a typhoon in the early 1800s, when the inhabitants of Satawal requested permission from the Spanish authorities to move a number of Carolinian refugees to that island. The permission was granted and the first settlment was established between 1815 and 1819 (Spoehr 1954: 70). At that time the island was otherwise uninhabited, since the native Chamorros had been moved to Guam in 1698 by the Spanish during their attempts to pacify the Marianas. Over the years, until 1870, other Carolinian migrants followed from Lamotrek, Satawal, and Namonuito. Chamorros did not begin to move back to the island until the 1860s. In 1865 there were only 9 Chamorros on Saipan compared to 424 Carolinians (Spoehr 1954: 71–72). The Chamorros apparently did not outnumber the Carolinians on this island until the German period of administration, that is, sometime between 1899 and 1914 after larger numbers of them moved from Guam to the northern Marianas.

The colonists from Satawal who settled on Saipan did not loose their rights to land on Satawal as a consequence of their move. Even today, several decades after separation, members of the Satawal community can point out the residences and affiliated land parcels that particular emigrants and their descendants have rights to if they should ever return to the island. In addition, the Satawalese usually claim they have rights to land on Saipan even though most have never seen the island. These claims derive not only from the fact that they have kin ties to the emigrants, but also by reference to the principle of priority of settlement, a principle of continuing importance in sorting out ownership rights and ranking within the central Carolines themselves (Alkire 1974). This was, after all, a time-tested rule of the coral islanders' adaptive strategy and it was only logical that they should extend the principle to Saipan as they did to all other areas they settled.

In contrast, the Saipan Carolinians and especially their descendants failed to retain a detailed knowledge of, or interest in, the coral island communities of the Carolines. Their perspective undoubtedly was an outgrowth of a difference in perceived needs and adaptive realities. Certainly there were great difficulties in maintaining communication between the two areas once direct voyaging ceased. But, in addition, adjustments were necessary within the Saipan Carolinian community that would facilitate both adaptation to this more productive and expansive high island, as well as to the competitive milieu of the wage economy that evolved on that island during Japanese times and after World War II. The Carolinians on Saipan were soon outnumbered by the Chamorros and the dominant Chamorro cultural context that developed encouraged younger Carolinians on the island to reject as "backward" their loincloth clad and tattooed coral island relatives in favor of emulation of the Western oriented and supposedly sophisticated Saipan and Guam Chamorros.

In the late 1960s and early 1970s Saipan Carolinian attitudes began to change as the result of discussions that were initiated between the Saipan government (Chamorro dominated) and the United States government. The purpose of the negotiation was to change the political status of the northern Marianas by removing these islands from the jurisdiction of the Trust Territory administration. The most forcefully discussed alternatives were either amalgamation with Guam or some more direct affiliation with the United States, since defined as Commonwealth status. The Saipan Carolinian community was far from enthusiastic about the implications of the first alternative since they believed that their interests would not be protected under any arrangement whereby their minority position vis-à-vis the Chamorros was increased. Even though they already were outnumbered by the Chamorros three to one they felt that their membership in the larger polity of the Trust Territory served to protect their basic rights. The Carolinians saw the possibility of being drowned by a new wave of Chamorro migration if Saipan should join Guam in some form of political union.

Consequently, the Saipan Carolinian leaders not only began to actively work against Guam–Saipan political unification, but also to work towards a revitalization of their cultural identity. Part of this revitalization involved looking for support among "newly rediscovered" relatives on their ancestral islands. A tactic that some Carolinians promoted was that of encouraging renewed migration from Satawal to Saipan, which they believed would ultimately increase the Carolinian political voice on the island. The residents of Satawal were receptive to these suggestions for they perceived that their own island would soon reach its carrying capacity—a reasonable conclusion since the population in 1970 was nearly 350 individuals and growing at a rate of between 2 and 3 percent per year.

With the encouragement of several influential members of the Saipan Carolinian community, then, the people of Satawal subsequently decided to resume direct contact and interisland voyaging to Saipan. On April 26, 1970 five Satawal men set sail from their island in a 26-foot sailing canoe for Saipan some 500 miles away. They arrived at Saipan on May 4th after a 4-day stopover on West Fayu en route and were enthusiastically greeted by the local Carolinian community. Three years later two more canoes repeated the feat. Both voyages symbolically were meant to strengthen Satawal claims to the island and precede actual renewed migration. Whether these ties will result in any long-term interdependence is doubtful, however, since political events appear to have overtaken the community. In mid-June 1975 the northern Marianas voters decided by a 78 percent majority to join the United States as a Commonwealth.

Modern transportation, then, has served in some cases to eliminate the isolation of many single coral islands, but in other instances, as among certain clusters and complexes, it has ironically reduced contact between some islands that traditionally had developed close ties through patterns of interisland canoe voyaging. In many of these latter cases, however, the memory of this former interdependence and its adaptive importance is easily revived given the right set of circumstances.

In most of the modern-day Pacific interaction networks now emphasize a port-town versus hinterland orientation (Spoehr 1960). This dyadic model seems especially appropriate for most of the coral islands of Polynesia and Micronesia. Today the Micronesian islands discussed in this book are inexorably tied to such port-towns as Kolonia on Ponape, Moen on Truk, Colonia, Yap and Ebeye or Majuro in the Marshalls. In Polynesia Papeete, Rarotonga, Apia, and, in some cases, the larger urban centers of Honolulu and Auckland influence even the most remote coral island.

Modern migration patterns bear this out. Increasingly large numbers of people are moving from the outer islands to the port-towns. For example, in the Marshall Islands at least 40 percent of the Marshallese now reside in either Ebeye or Majuro. We have already noted that 50 percent of the Pukapukans now live in New Zealand. This type of migration has resulted not only in the establishment of "daughter communities" but also, because of its magnitude, in squatter villages of coral islanders that are often localized on the fringes of a port-town, the residents of which are subject to the discrimination and exploitation of the larger community. These migrants inevitably are closely tied to the local unskilled wage labor market. As that market grows, larger numbers of migrants are attracted to the port-town, but conversely as wage labor opportunities decrease it often happens that a comparable number of migrants do not return to their outer island homes. Rather the squatter community finds it must accommodate an ever-growing population on increasingly marginal resources. The fascination and activity of the port-town acts as a magnet even in the face of a decreasing standard of living.

In "good" wage labor times the port-town residents may send part of their wages back to relatives on their home atolls, which of course only serves to attract ever more migrants. In "bad" wage labor times the port-town residents may begin to drain home islands of some of their limited resources—money from copra sales or in some cases even food. Most of the migrants to the port-towns are able-bodied young or middle aged males, for these are the individuals needed by the wage labor market. The outer islands, then, often are left with populations composed of disproportionately large numbers of females, the aged, and the very young. With large numbers of able-bodied males absent, such communities are top-heavy with consumers and short of producers; this obviously places great strains on the coral island community even in times when additional demands are not made by the migrants.

When copra prices decline patterns of interdependence are further replaced by patterns of dependence, wherein the outer islands continue to survive as viable communities only if supported or subsidized by the port-town. Subsidized shipping lines, medical care, schooling and in some cases food supplies serve to maintain those outlying communities that no longer engage in viable subsistence production themselves. Ironically this "drain" most often was first fostered by the port-town itself when its administrators and traders began their push towards commercial production among the outer islanders. The vagaries of commercial markets soon begin to take a toll among outer islanders and the higher material standard of living promised by commercialism most often is only realized by a minority of port-town residents. In those few cases where outer islands have prospered it has invariably been achieved in strong market times and at the expense of self-sufficiency.

What is the future for coral island communities? The world economic and political crises of the recent past—the Great Depression and World War II—have affected residents of port-towns more seriously than those outer islands that retained a degree of self-sufficiency and subsistence emphasis. This obviously follows from the fact that these outer islanders were less closely tied to the world economic scene. Collapsing prices, as in a depression, or interrupted shipping, as during a war, are inconveniences that are overcome by greater emphasis on subsistence production. In contrast within the port-towns these same circumstances may bring the populace to the brink of starvation.

Today on most Polynesian and Micronesian coral islands commercial production is replacing subsistence horticulture, outboard motors are replacing sails, and population pyramids resemble hourglasses. At the time of this writing copra prices have begun to fall, and, at the same time that money is becoming scarce, the prices of imported foodstuffs and gasoline are rising. Unless there is a revitalization in subsistence horticulture and maritime exploitation there is a very real possibility that the standard of living for many coral islanders will further decline. The two other options are increased subsidization and more rapid abandonment of the hinterland in favor of the port-town.

Most coral island communities of the past have survived resource shortages and population displacements with adaptive strategies that maximized options. The most successful communities described in this book appear to have been those that further emphasized island interdependence. If viable coral island communities are to survive into the future, there probably will have to be a revitalization of this basic strategy.

BIBLIOGRAPHY

Alkire, W. H.
  1977 *An Introduction to the Peoples and Cultures of Micronesia.* Second edition. Cummings Publ. Co., Menlo Park, Calif.

  1974 "Land Tenure in the Woleai," chapter 3 in *Land Tenure in Oceania* (ed. by H. P. Lundsgaarde). University Press of Hawaii.

  1972 "Concepts of Order in Southeast Asia and Micronesia," *Comparative Studies in Society and History,* 14:484–493.

  1970 "Systems of Measurement on Woleai Atoll, Caroline Islands," *Anthropos,* 65:1–73.

  1968 "Porpoises and Taro," *Ethnology* 7:280–289.

  1965 *Lamotrek Atoll and Inter-island Socioeconomic Ties.* Illinois Studies in Anthropology, No. 5. University of Illinois Press.

Barrau, Jacques
  1958 *Subsistence Agriculture in Melanesia.* B. P. Bishop Museum Bulletin No. 219. Honolulu.

Bayliss-Smith, Tim
  1974 "Constraints on Population Growth: The Case of the Polynesian Outlier Atolls in the Precontact Period," *Human Ecology,* 2(4):259–295.

Beaglehole, Ernest and Pearl Beaglehole
    1938 *Ethnology of Pukapuka.* B. P. Bishop Museum Bulletin
          No. 150. Honolulu.

Bellwood, Peter
    1975 "The Prehistory of Oceania," *Current Anthropology,*
          16:9–28.

Bryan, E. H.
    1970 *Land in Micronesia and Its Resources.* Pacific Scientific
          Information Center. B. P. Bishop Museum, Honolulu.

Buck, Peter
    1932a *Ethnology of Tongareva.* B. P. Bishop Museum Bulletin
          No. 92. Honolulu.

    1932b *Ethnology of Manihiki and Rakahanga.* B. P. Bishop Mu-
          seum Bulletin No. 99. Honolulu.

Carroll, Vern (editor)
    1975 *Pacific Atoll Populations.* The University Press of Hawaii.
          Honolulu.

Catala, R. L. A.
    1957 "Report on the Gilbert Islands: Some Aspects of Human
          Ecology," *Atoll Research Bulletin,* No. 59.

Crocombe, Ron
    1971 *Land Tenure in the Pacific.* Oxford University Press.

Dahl, A. L., B. C. Patten, S. Smith, and J. Zieman, Jr.
    1974 "A Preliminary Coral Reef Ecosystem Model," in *Compar-
          ative Investigations of Tropical Reef Ecosystems* (ed. by M.
          H. Sachet and A. L. Dahl), *Atoll Research Bulletin,* No.
          172.

Danielsson, Bengt
    1956 *Work and Life on Raroia.* George Allen and Unwin, Lon-
          don.

Darwin, Charles
    1901 (first edition, 1842) *The Structure and Distribution of
          Coral Reefs.* 3rd ed. D. Appleton, London.

Davenport, William
    1975 "The Population of the Outer Reef Islands, British Solo-
          mon Islands Protectorate," chapter 3 in *Pacific Atoll Popu-
          lations* (edited by Vern Carroll). The University Press of
          Hawaii, Honolulu.

1960 "Marshall Islands Navigational Charts," *Imago Mundi* 15:19–26.

Davis, W. M.
1928 *The Coral Reef Problem.* American Geographical Society Special Publication No. 9. New York.

Degener, Otto
1930 *Plants of Hawaii National Park.* Honolulu Star Bulletin Press.

Dyen, Isadore
1965 *A Lexicostatistical Classification of the Austronesian Languages.* International Journal of American Linguistics Memoir, No. 19. Indiana University Press.

Emory, K. P.
1975 *Material Culture of the Tuamotu Archipelago.* Pacific Anthropological Records, No. 22. B. P. Bishop Museum, Honolulu.
1965 *Kapingamarangi: Social and Religious Life on a Polynesian Atoll.* B. P. Bishop Museum Bulletin, No. 228. Honolulu.
1934 *Archaeology of the Pacific Equatorial Islands.* B. P. Bishop Museum Bulletin, No. 123. Honolulu.

Gifford, E. W. and D. S. Gifford
1959 *Archaeological Excavations in Yap.* Anthropological Records, Vol. 18, No. 2. University of California, Berkeley.

Golson, J.
1962 "Polynesian Navigation," Part II, table II, *Journal of the Polynesian Society,* 71(4):79–154.

Goodenough, W. H.
1957 "Oceania and the Problem of Controls in the Study of Cultural and Human Evolution," *Journal of the Polynesian Society.* 66:146–155.
1955 "A Problem in Malayo-Polynesian Social Organization," *American Anthropologist,* 57:71–83.

Grace, George
1961 "Austronesian Linguistics and Culture History," *American Anthropologist,* 63:359–368.

Grimble, Sir Arthur
1957 *Return to the Islands.* Murray, London.

Haddon, A. C. and John Hornell
1936 *The Canoes of Oceania.* 2 vols. B. P. Bishop Museum Special Publication, No. 27. Honolulu.

Hatanaka, S.
1972 "The Settlement and Population in Pukarua," unpublished paper read at Atoll Population Conference, East-West Center.

Hooper, Antony and Judith Huntsman
1973 "A Demographic History of the Tokelau Islands," *Journal of the Polynesian Society,* 82:366–411.

Howells, W. W.
1973 *The Pacific Islanders.* Scribners, New York.

Hunt, E. E., N. R. Kidder, and D. M. Schneider
1954 "The Depopulation of Yap," *Human Biology,* 26:21–51.

Japanese Government
1931–37 Nanyo-cho. (Censuses of the Mandated Territories).

Knudson, K. E.
1970 *Resource Fluctuation, Productivity, and Social Organization on Micronesian Coral Islands.* Unpublished Ph.D. thesis, University of Oregon, Eugene.

Kotzebue, Otto von
1821 *A Voyage of Discovery into the South Sea and Beering's Straights . . . 1815–1818.* Vol. 3. Phillips, London.

Krämer, Augustin
1917 *Palau.* Ergebnisse der Südsee Expedition 1908–1910. II, Band 3, Pt. 1. Hamburg.
1937 *Zentralkarolinen.* Ergebnisse der Südsee Expedition 1908–1910. II, Band 10, Pt. 1. Hamburg.

Lambert, Bernd
1971 "The Gilbert Islands," chapter 8 in *Land Tenure in the Pacific* (ed. by R. Crocombe). Oxford University Press.

Lamont, E. H.
1867 *Wild Life among the Pacific Islanders.* Hurst and Blackett, London.

Lawton, J. H.
1973 "The Energy Cost of 'Food-Gathering'," Pp. 59–76 in *Resources and Population* (ed. by B. Benjamin *et al*). Academic Press, London.

Lessa, William
    1964 "The Social Effects of Typhoon Ophelia (1960) on Ulithi,"
        Micronesica, 1:1–47.
    1962 "An Evaluation of Early Descriptions of Carolinian Cul-
        ture," *Ethnohistory*, 9:313–404.
    1955 "Depopulation on Ulithi," *Human Biology*, 27:161–183.
    1950 "Ulithi and the Outer Native World," *American An-
        thropologist*, 52:27–52.

Lessa, William and G. C. Myers
    1962 "Population Dynamics of an Atoll Community," *Popula-
        tion Studies*, 15:244–257.

Levin, Michael
    1976 *Eauripik Population Structure.* Unpublished Ph.D. thesis.
        University of Michigan, Ann Arbor.

Levison, M., R. G. Ward, and J. W. Webb
    1973 *The Settlement of Polynesia: A Computer Simulation.* Uni-
        versity of Minnesota Press.

Lieber, Michael D.
    1974 "Land Tenure on Kapingamarangi," chapter 4 in *Land
        Tenure in Oceania* (ed. by H. Lundsgaarde). University
        Press of Hawaii.
    1968 *Porakiet: A Kapingamarangi Colony on Ponape.* Depart-
        ment of Anthropology, University of Oregon, Eugene.

Leob, Edwin M.
    1926 *History and Traditions of Niue.* B. P. Bishop Museum Bul-
        letin, No. 32. Honolulu.

McArthur, N., I. W. Saunders, and R. L. Tweedie
    1976 "Small Population Isolates, A Micro-simulation Study,"
        Journal of the Polynesian Society, 85:307–326.

MacGregor, Gordon
    1937 *Ethnology of the Tokelau Islands.* B. P. Bishop Museum
        Bulletin, No. 146. Honolulu.

Mason, Leonard
    1968 "Suprafamilial Authority and Economic Process in Mi-
        cronesian Atolls," chapter 16 in *Peoples and Cultures of
        the Pacific* (ed. by A. P. Vayda). Natural History Press,
        Garden City, N.Y.
    1954 *Relocation of the Bikini Marshallese.* Unpublished Ph.D.
        thesis. Yale.

Meller, Norman
 1969 *The Congress of Micronesia.* The University of Hawaii Press.

Murdock, G. P.
 1948 "Anthropology in Micronesia," *New York Academy of Sciences Transactions,* Series 2, 11:9–16.

Newell, N. D.
 1972 "The Evolution of Reefs," *Scientific American,* 226(6):54–65.

Osborne, Douglas
 1966 *The Archaeology of the Palau Islands.* B. P. Bishop Museum Bulletin, No. 230. Honolulu.

Ottino, Paul
 1972 "Demography and Social Structure in Rangiroa, Tuamotus," unpublished paper presented at Atoll Population Conference, East-West Center, Honolulu.

 1970 "Adoption on Rangiroa Atoll, Tuamotu Archipelago," chapter 5 in *Adoption in Eastern Oceania* (ed. by V. Carroll), University of Hawaii Press.

 1967 "Early 'Ati of the Western Tuamotus," in *Polynesian Culture History* (ed. by G. Highland *et al*), B. P. Bishop Museum Special Publication, No. 56. Honolulu.

Percival. W. H.
 1974 "Pukapuka: Remote but Changing," *Pacific Islands Monthly,* August, page 61.

Pirie, Peter
 1972 "Population Growth in the Pacific Islands," chapter 8 in *Man in the Pacific Islands* (ed. by R. Ward), Clarendon Press, Oxford.

Riesenberg, Saul
 1965 "Table of Voyages Affecting Micronesian Islands," *Oceania,* 36(2):155–170.

Sahlins, Marshall
 1958 *Social Stratification in Polynesia.* American Ethnological Society, University of Washington Press.

Shutler, Richard, Jr., and M. E. Shutler
 1975 *Oceanic Prehistory.* Cummings, Menlo Park, Calif.

Spoehr, Alexander
1960 "Port Town and Hinterland in the Pacific Islands," *American Anthropologist*, 62:586–592.

1957 *Marianas Prehistory*. Fieldiana, No. 48. Chicago Natural History Museum.

1954 *Saipan: The Ethnology of a War Devastated Island*. Fieldiana, No. 41. Chicago Natural History Museum.

Stone, Benjamin
1970 *The Flora of Guam*. Micronesica, vol. 6. University of Guam.

Thompson, Laura
1970 "A Self-Regulating System of Human Population Control," *Transactions of the New York Academy of Sciences*, Series II, Vol. 32, No. 1, pp. 262–270.

1949 "The Relations of Men, Animals, and Plants in an Island Community (Fiji)," *American Anthropologist*, 51(2):253–267.

Tobin, J. A.
1958 "Land Tenure in the Marshall Islands," chapter in *Land Tenure Patterns, Trust Territory of the Pacific Islands* (ed. by J. de Young). Office of the High Commissioner of the Trust Territory of the Pacific Islands. Guam.

Tracey, J. I., D. P. Abbott, and T. Arnow
1961 *Natural History of Ifaluk Atoll*. B. P. Bishop Museum Bulletin, No. 222. Honolulu.

United States State Department
1951–72 Annual Reports to the United Nations on the Trust Territory of the Pacific Islands.

Vayda, A. P.
1959 "Polynesian Cultural Distributions in New Perspective," *American Anthropologist*, 61:817–828.

Vayda, A. P., and R. Rappaport
1962 "Island Cultures," chapter in *Man's Place in the Island Ecosystem* (ed. by F. R. Fosberg). B. P. Bishop Museum. Honolulu.

Wedgwood, Camilla
1936 "Report on Research Work in Nauru Island, Central Pacific," *Oceania*, 6:359–361, 7:1–33.

Walmsley, D. J.
  1972 *Systems Theory: A Framework for Human Geographical Enquiry.* Australian National University.

Wiens, Herold
  1962 *Atoll Environment and Ecology.* Yale University Press.

Wilson, William *et al.*
  1799 *A Missionary Voyage to the South Pacific Ocean.* Chapman, London.

GLOSSARY OF NATIVE AND SCIENTIFIC TERMS

Adze. A hafted cutting tool, the blade of which is mounted at right angles to the handle.

Alocasia macrorrhiza. A large tropical plant with satittate-ovate leaves, perhaps 60 cm long with tips pointing down. Its tuberous roots are edible when cooked but if eaten raw are irritating and painful, owing to crystals of calcium oxalate contained in the uncooked tissues.

Amenengame (Nauru). Commoners.

Ariki (Manihiki-Rakahanga). Chiefly rank.

Aroid. A collective term used to describe a number of tuberous root crops such as Cyrtosperma, Colocasia, and Alocasia.

Arrowroot. *Tacca sp.* A perennial herb with white, starchy tubers.

'ati (Tuamotus). A bilateral (ambilineal) descent group; a ramage.

Austronesian. The language family or phylum that includes most of the languages of Indonesia, Melanesia, Micronesia, and Polynesia. Synonymous with Malayo-Polynesian.

Breadfruit. *Artocarpus incisus, altilis,* and *mariannensis.* A large tropical tree with edible fruit when cooked. The tree also provides a good quality soft wood.

Bwe (Woleai). A system of divination involving the counting of knots tied in strips taken from coconut frond pinnae.

Bwij (Marshalls). A matrilineal descent line.

Bwogot (Woleai). An estate, the land, and its people. Often synonymous with "my relatives or kinsmen."

Bwulikul (Woleai). Excavation of a taro field.

Bwulog (Woleai). *Cyrtosperma chamissonis.*

Calophyllum inophyllum. A large tropical tree with broad crown and ovate leaves. It is a strand plant providing a deep colored, hard wood of excellent quality.

Cassytha. A vine-like parasitic plant, commonly found along beaches.

Chamorro. The native language and inhabitants of the Mariana Islands.

Chanos chanos. Milkfish. A herring-like fish up to 3 feet in length, but more commonly less than 1 foot long whose fry are frequently caught along beaches and transferred to brackish ponds for raising and later harvesting.

Cho (Woleai). A mature or ripe coconut or the meat of a ripe coconut.

Chúlifeimag. (Woleai). An intra-atoll exchange system.

Chúlim (Woleai). A consecrated set of mountain apple leaves used in the post-partum purification ceremony.

Colocasia esculenta. A common domestic plant of tropical Asia and the Pacific. Its leaves are ovate-cordate, tips pointing down. It provides an edible tuberous root of starchy potato-like food of purplish color.

Copra. The dried salable meat of mature coconuts. The source of coconut oil.

Cordia subcordata. A small tree, 1 to 12 meters tall with ovate pale green leaves. A strand species with good quality wood.

Crataeva sp. A small to moderate-sized tree that bears an olive-green, white-speckled fruit similar in size to a mango (but unrelated). The fruit is characterized by a somewhat pungent flavor and can be eaten raw or cooked.

Crown-of-thorn starfish. *Acanthaster planci.* A large starfish with sharp spines that inhabits tropical reefs and consumes the living reef organisms.

Cyrtosperma chamissonis. A moderate-sized tropical plant with ovate-sagtittate leaves perhaps more than 1 meter in length, pointing upward. It possesses an edible tuberous root generally of yellow color.

Dioscorea alata. Yams. A vine-like plant with large starchy tubers. A common food crop on volcanic Pacific islands.

Edongo (Nauru). Preserved pandanus.

Equatorial trough. The shallow trough of low pressure, generally situated near the equator, marking the convergence zone of air which moves towards the equator from the subtropical anticyclones of either hemisphere. The trough over the Pacific lies in the belt of the doldrums and has a north and south movement which follows the sun with a time-lag of one to two months.

Fafa (Woleai).   Rainbow runners. A pelagic fish.

Falubwa (Woleai).   The sap from a coconut tree that has been tapped for consumption either sweet or fermented.

Fara (Tuamotus).   Pandanus.

Fät (Woleai).   To plant a crop; also seeds.

Feifei (Woleai).   To weed a garden.

Fekafekau (Niue).   Commoners.

Gailang (Woleai).   A matrilineal clan.

Galigi (Woleai).   A ceremony to increase the productivity of taro.

Ghyben-Hertzberg lens.   The source of fresh groundwater on atoll islands.

Guettarda.   A small tree or shrub with broad ovate leaves 10 to 15 cm long. The plant possesses small white or pink flowers that are pollinated at night by moths and that fall in the morning. A strand species.

Hachi (Woleai).   The sap collected from a coconut tree for consumption, usually after fermentation.

Halving.   The process common to Woleai ideational culture whereby social, political, or material units are divided into halves, usually in order to maintain a ceremonial or ritual balance.

Harangap (Woleai).   *Katsuwonus pelamis.* A small bonito or tuna.

Haria (Woleai).   A fine levied for violation of a taboo.

Holas (Woleai).   The first assistant or "chancellor" of a chief.

Hophopilifal (Woleai).   A food gift made in honor of a deceased man at the time a canoe house he utilized is first rethatched following his death.

Hů (Woleai).   "Fishhook," an interisland tribute and exchange system involving Lamotrek, Elato, and Satawal islands.

Hubwulimäs (Woleai).   "Party for the dead," a funeral feast.

Hulihuli (Woleai).   To harvest Colocasia.

Hurricane.   A large circulating tropical storm with sustained surface winds of 64 knots or more located east of the 180° meridan.

-iaf (Woleai).   A counting suffix referring to a grouping of objects, ceremonially computed as 10 but actually containing 8.

igalifelu (Woleai).   "Fish of the island," a share of fish offered as part of the intra-atoll exchange system.

Intertropical convergence zone.   A relatively narrow, low-latitude zone in which air masses originating in the two hemispheres converge. Over the Pacific the zone is the boundary between the northeasterly and south-easterly trade winds.

Itsio (Nauru).   Serfs.

Kainga (Tongareva). Lands of a ramage, an estate.

Kanava (Tokelau). *Cordia subcordata.*

Kasig (Woleai). Dances performed at a female puberty ceremony. Synonym: *huluhul.*

Lalo tagata (Niue). "Low people," serfs.

Lamotrekalaplap (Woleai). "Greater Lamotrek," i.e. Lamotrek, Elato, and Satawal, the islands of the *hù.*

Legot (Woleai). A female puberty ceremony, the young girl herself.

Malayo-Polynesian. A language family or phylum including most of the languages of Indonesia, Micronesia, Melanesia, and Polynesia. Synonymous with Austronesian.

Mar (Woleai). Preserved, fermented breadfruit.

Marae (Manihiki-Rakahanga). A shrine.

Masanga (Tongareva). A type of taboo that prohibited exploitation of designated coconut trees.

Matakeinanga (Manihiki-Rakahanga). A descent group, ramage.

Mbuc (Yap). A native valuable of banana fiber cloth.

Megalithic complex. A presumed wide-spread cultural complex of Asia and the Pacific characterized by large scale stone constructions.

Messerschmidia. A small shrub or tree 5 to 6 meters tall with silvery, fleshy leaves. An Indo-Pacific strand plant.

Milkfish. *Chanos chanos.*

Mountain apple. *Eugenia javanica.* A moderate to large tree that bears, in appearance, an apple-like small red fruit.

Mushang (Woleai). A taboo sign placed by an offended party on an object he intends to confiscate if he is not paid a fine *(haria).*

Pandanus. Screw pine. A tree with aerial prop roots, long sword-like leaves, often toothed with spines. The tree bears a large fruit with fibrous edible yellow pericarp.

Patuiki (Niue). Paramount chief.

Pelagic fish. A free swimming, open ocean variety of fish, commonly called blue water fish.

Pelu (Woleai). A traditionally trained native navigator.

Pemphis. A shrub or small tree with thick branches, oblong-elliptic fleshy leaves. A common strand species in Indo-Pacific areas.

Pisonia. A soft wooded tree with short, stocky trunk and ovate pale thin leaves. Common to strand areas of the Pacific.

Proto-Malayo-Polynesian. The hypothesized linguistic and cultural antecedent family that gave rise to Malayo-Polynesian/Austronesian.

Pule. (Pukapuka). Guards (and their authority) who protected reserve lands from theft of produce.

Puna (Manihiki-Rakahanga). A kindred or "family."

Ragash (Woleai). *Calophyllum inophyllum.*

Ragum (Woleai). A species of terrestrial crabs.

Rainbow runner. Hawaiian salmon, *Elagatis bipinnulatus.* A moderate-sized pelagic fish.

Rang (Woleai). *Curcuma,* turmeric. The yellow powder made from an herb, valued as a cosmetic for its color and odor.

Rop (Woleai). A group fishing technique, using surround nets and frond screens.

Sapet (Woleai). A period of mourning established by a chief after a death, during which the community is prohibited from harvesting coconuts.

Sawei (Woleai). An interisland sociopolitical and economic exchange system among the people of the islands of the central Carolines and Yap.

Scaevola. An erect, soft-wooded, moderate-sized shrub with fleshy leaves native to rocky and strand beaches in the Indo-Pacific area.

Sennit. The processed fiber of coconut husks used in manufacture of cordage.

Shufelu (Woleai). An important all-islands meeting at which a new chief is installed and the funeral restrictions that were in effect since the death of the former chief are removed.

Shùwar (Woleai). A post-partum purification ceremony.

Star compass. The square navigational compass concept, based on star positions, used by Carolinian navigators.

Strand species. Those plant species native to sandy beach areas, usually highly salt tolerant.

Sweet potatoes. *Ipomoea batatas.* A small white sweet potato similar in appearance to an Irish potato.

Tairang (Woleai). Female puberty ceremony.

Tamol (Woleai). A chief.

Tei (Woleai). A general meeting or a meeting of chiefs.

Temonibe (Nauru). Nobility.

Toa (Niue). Warriors.

Tsunami. A seismic wave, commonly called a tidal wave.

Tugatug (Woleai). A wrapping. A piece of cloth intended for a shroud offered as a gift at a funeral ceremony.

Tur (Woleai). A traditional loom-woven skirt or loincloth of banana or hibiscus fiber.

Turtles. In Micronesia this generally refers to the great green sea turtle (*Chelonia* sp.).

Typhoon. A large circulating, counterclockwise in the Northern hemisphere, tropical storm with sustained surface winds of 64 knots or more. Found west of the 180th meridian.

Ubwut (Woleai). The newly emerged immature frond of a coconut tree before the pinnae have separated. When the leaves are pulled apart the pinnae are a bright yellow color.

Ulaam (Woleai). A type of small basket fish trap, plaited from split bamboo or similar type of wood.

Uòt (Woleai). *Colocasia esculenta.*

Walnibwúl (Woleai). Mulching of a taro garden.

Wato (Marshalls). A land division, an estate.

Wugulibwúl (Woleai). To harvest *Cyrtosperma.*

Yalus (Woleai). A ghost, spirit, or god.

Yar (Yap). A valuable of mother-of-pearl shell, decorated by attaching a sennit fiber handle.

Index

Abemama Island, 67
Abortion, 74, 82, 91, 93, 110
Adoption, 97, 106, 136
Ailinglapalap Island, 133
Alkire, William H., 40, 43, 48, 51, 53, 122, 130, 131, 142
Alocasia, 26, 103, 106, 112
Amanu Island, 105
'Ana'a Island, 107
Angaur Island, 66
Aranuka Island, 67, 109
Arno Island, 11, 17, 132, 133
Aroids, *see* Colocasia; Cyrtosperma
Arorae Island, 67
Arrowroot, 26, 31, 80, 103, 132
'Arutua Island, 105
Atafu Island, 67, 98–103, 108–109

Banaba Island, 11–13, 17, 67, 138
Bananas, 26, 31, 80
Barrau, Jacques, 30
Barrier reefs, 6
Bats, 18
Bayliss-Smith, Tim, 29, 30
Beaglehole, Ernest, 30, 86, 88, 89
Beaglehole, Pearl, 86, 88, 89
Bellwood, Peter, 20
Bikini Island, 12, 17, 132
Birds, 10, 18
Birth rate, 31, 74
Breadfruit, 26, 31, 37, 45, 55, 72, 80, 100, 112, 132, 134
Bryan, E. H., 33
Buck, Peter, 83, 85, 94, 96–98
Butaritari Island, 12, 67, 109
Byron, John, 100

Canoes, 23–26, 81, 83, 90, 115, 133
Canton Island, 11
Caroline Islands, 7, 68, 112–131, 134–135, 140–141
  houses, 22, 23
  population, 31, 34, 39
  rainfall, 12
  settlement, 21
  typhoons, 14
  See also specific islands
Catala, R. L. A., 74
Central Caroline Islands, *see* Caroline Islands

Chamorros, 141–143
Cheyne, Andrew, 36
Climate, *see* Droughts; Rainfall; Typhoons
Clusters, 66, 67, 94–111, 140, 144
Coconuts, 26, 27, 30–31, 72, 80, 83, 88, 96, 100, 102, 103, 112, 114, 132, 137–138
Colocasia, 26, 27, 30, 45, 83, 88, 103, 112, 134
Competition, 77–78, 90
Complexes, 66, 67–68, 112–136, 140, 144
Cook Islands, *see* Northern Cook Islands
Cooking house, 44
Coral islands and atolls
  canoes, 23–26, 81, 83, 90, 115, 133
  clusters, 66, 67, 94–111, 140, 144
  complexes, 66, 67–68, 112–136, 140, 144
  crops, 26–27, 30–31, 37, 45, 55, 72, 80, 83, 88, 90, 96, 100, 102, 103, 106, 112, 114, 132, 134, 137–138
  cultural background, 39, 40
  daily activities, 41–68
  droughts, 11–12, 14, 15, 17, 29, 70, 72, 74, 76, 80, 81, 86, 100
  elevation, 3–7, 14–16
  emerging structures, 137–146
  erosion, 9
  fauna, 18
  fishing, 1, 23, 27, 28, 45, 47, 55–57, 60, 63, 72, 76, 81, 83, 146
  formation, 3–7, 9
  horticulture, 27–28, 45, 55, 58, 63, 73, 76, 80, 112, 132, 146
  houses, 22–23, 43–44
  isolates, 2, 18, 65–67, 69–73, 137–140, 144
  kin groups, 40, 72, 83, 85, 88, 91, 105–106, 116–117
  labor, division of, 45, 56, 60–61, 63, 114
  land ownership, 72–74, 76–77, 81, 90–91, 97, 101, 142
  marine species, 1, 18
  marriage, 74, 76, 81, 91, 97, 105–106, 124–127
  navigation, 115–116, 132–133, 140
  political affairs, 64, 82, 92, 109, 117–118, 130, 132–134, 140